AF433911

Title page
Money, **Money, MONEY,**

The Real Pandemic,
The 1%
(The ORIGINAL drawing
with poetry and comment)
By STEVEN SELBY

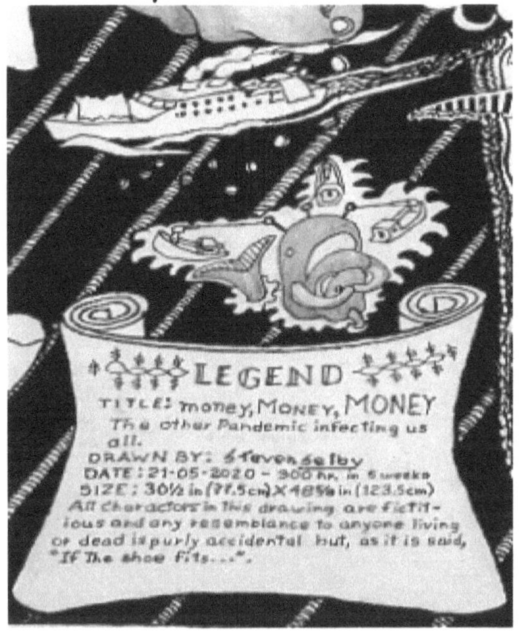

Money, Money, Money, The 1%

Steven Selby

Published by Steven Selby, 2024.

While every precaution has been taken in the preparation of this book, the publisher assumes no responsibility for errors or omissions, or for damages resulting from the use of the information contained herein.

MONEY, MONEY, MONEY, THE 1%

First edition. March 21, 2024.

Copyright © 2024 Steven Selby.

ISBN: 979-8224041725

Written by Steven Selby.

Also by Steven Selby

Money, Money, Money, The 1%

Table of Contents

LEFT-HAND PANEL

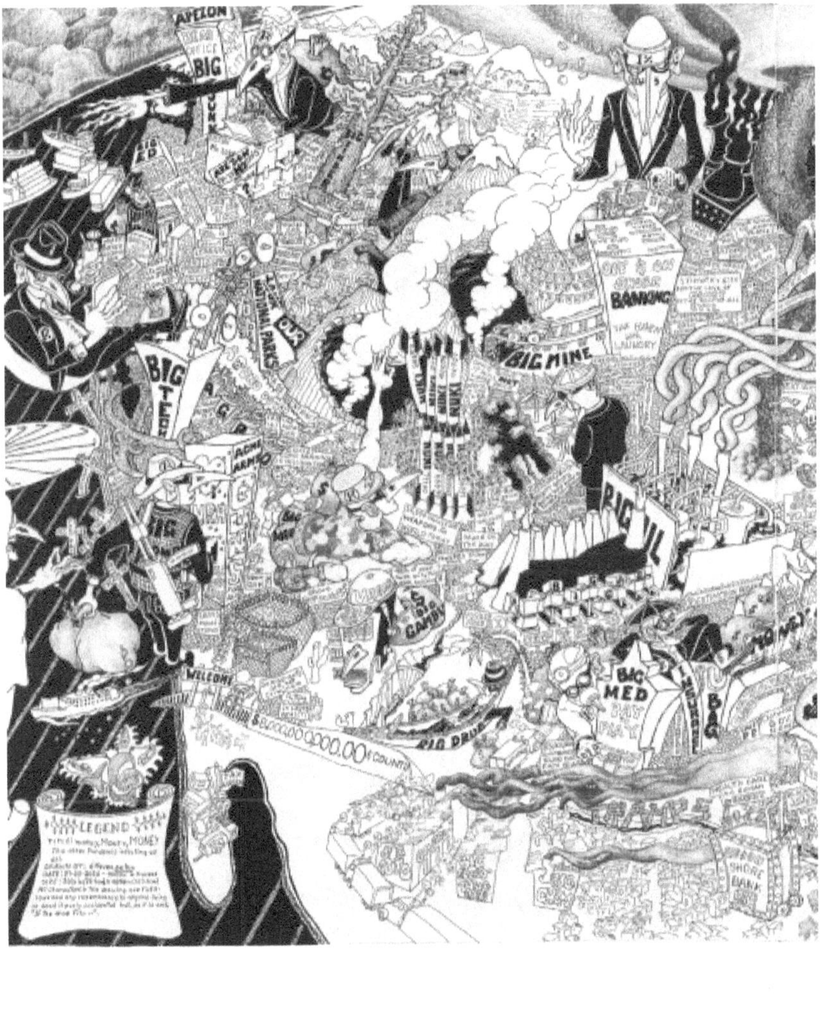

RIGHT-HAND PANEL

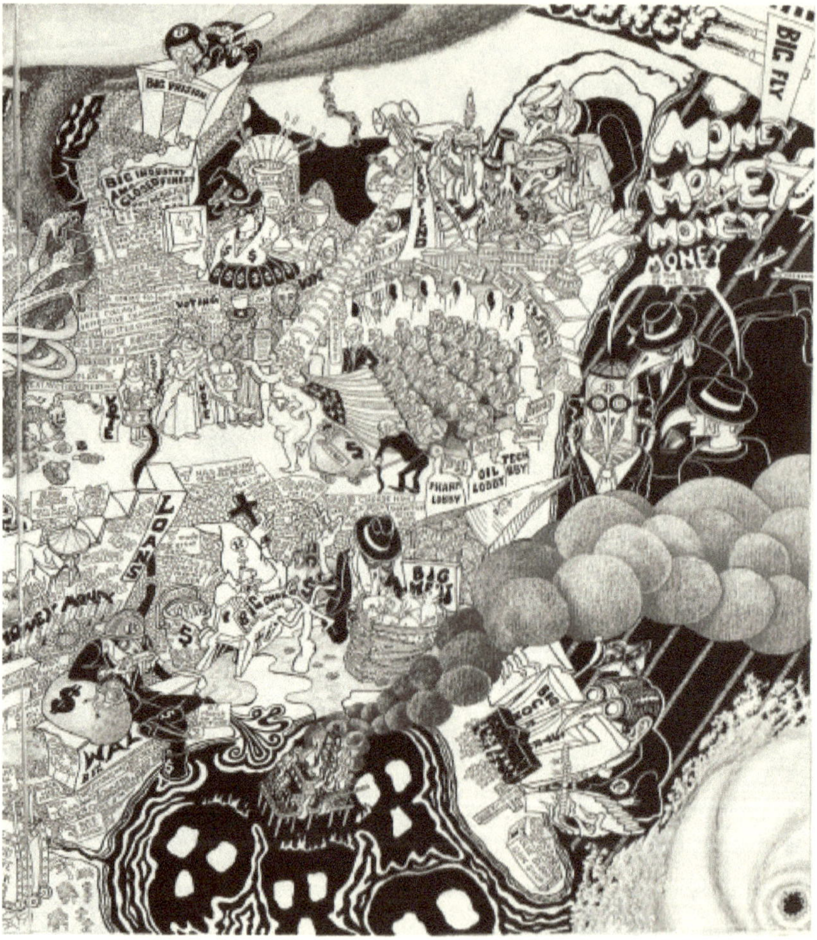

INTRODUCTION (2020)

The year is 2020 and the world is in a heightened state of turmoil due to a plague of a Coronavirus named COVID-19 which by the end of its first year will have killed over 200,000 and spread to millions of people worldwide. The ultimate effect of this plague may take a long time to play out but its effects will most assuredly be widespread. What that ultimate effect will be is the subject of much debate because it is occurring at a very troubling political and economic period. There are numerous discussions on Capitalism, for and against,

Leading up to the first concerns about Covid 19, I had been trying to find a 'big picture' approach to the ills of Capitalism, and along came Berny Sanders a long-time Senator in the US Congress who ran for the nomination for President of the United States in 2016. He is the first US politician I ever heard who expressed thoughts on the ills of Capitalism that I agree with. Since 2016 the political dialog of the US and the world has shifted some in the direction of Bernie's dialect. We are not there yet but, moving in that direction. I for one, with millions of others, am feeling our way along this path. By the early months of 2020 when the Caronaviras raised its ugly head the politics of the US looked as if the people had begun to see more clearly what capitalism was doing to the nation and the Western World but the Coronavirus and the election of Donald Trump put a quick ending to that movement.

In the first month of 'lockdown' the idea for my drawing 'Money' came to me. At first, I wanted to do a large mural but my wife and daughter pointed out that if we were to move from where we were living it might be difficult to carry a large stone wall with us. Even though we were living in a very small wooden house with walls of crudely cut wood, plan "B" quickly became black ink on paper which I had on hand.

As the progress of the pandemic accelerated, images of what Covid 19 might look like started to appear, and though I had never associated Capitalism with a disease, the idea of the malicious pandemic seemed to fit very well. After all, one of the most traumatic events of history was the 14th and 15th-century plagues that brought devastation to the European world much like Capitalism has brought to our present world. It also seemed right to depict the US as the center of these ills since it has been the central motivator of the capitalist world and seemed to be leading the reaction to COVID-19 and it seems to be the home base for many of the world's riches and greediest. I should add that 2020 was an election year in the US which would most likely bring the influence of the rich face-to-face with the poor.

The problems of Wrold's economic system are many and mighty and a huge mural would have been more effective in bringing out all of the different influences it has on our life but that wasn't practical at the time. In reducing the size of the design I had also to reduce the scope of what I could depict. So this drawing, Money, is meant to be just one of a series of Cartoons illustrating the depth of the problems our current economic system has brought to the world. I think that mankind's most ancient intuition is that Money is the root of all evil and in the bible, we are told this in 1 Timothy 6:10 "For the love of money is the root of all evil". I could see no better place to start, and as I have pointed out, Bernie Sanders has given us a long list of examples that help illustrate this evil. I sometimes think that humans are indeed like the three monkeys when it comes to evil where they can not see, hear, or speak of evil until the whole planet and the life on it is trashed to the point of no return. It follows that the more money you have the less interest in any changes to the system you will have.

So, the full title of my Cartoon is, "money, Money, MONEY - The Real Pandemic - 1%". It was my hope the drawing would shout above the clammer of cars, the pumping of oil wells, the sound of airplanes polluting, and the screaming of endless wars, to get your attention. Here then is what Bernie calls the One Percent which comes from the fact that 1% (about 26 people) of the population has accumulated the same amount of wealth as about 60% (2.8 billion) of the world's poorest. The drawing was made in 2020 but this testament of relative wealth seems to be holding up, unfortunately well. The villains in my story are the 1% and I intend to point out the obscenities of their wealth and the effects the imbalance of wealth is having on our country, During the plagues, the "death doctors" as they became known, were depicted in the art of the time dressed in a mask that was a bag hanging over the nose and mouth and thick glasses to protect the eyes from the entree of the disease and help hold the mask in place. In the art of these times, there were no cameras, the doctors were very sinister characters and wore wide-brimmed hats and black capes. I have chosen to dress my 1%ers in their expensive suits unless they are known by a particular form of attire and headgear that might help identify them but have tried not to make them into a sinister element in my story to allow my viewers to make their judgments, I have provided masks for all of my 1%ers. As I have already pointed out it is not my intention to demean individuals but to explore the follies of our very outdated capitalism. As they used to say in the old days of radio, "All characters in this drawing are fictitious and any resemblance to anyone living or dead is purely accidental" but, as it is also said, "If the shoe fits....".

The largest part of the story of Capitalism is surely how it has affected all of us who are not among the rich of the world. Due to the constraints of a drawing, even a large one, I am not able to address this in depth but have tried to represent some of the many views of the 60% by using the handmade signs used by protestors. The little circles that make up the entire background of the drawing represent the huge human movement needed for change. In 2020 the pandemic has increased the very real need for mass demonstrations. It is no longer just Police brutality that is a determent to legally guaranteed rights of assembly and protest, it is now a health concern.

SECOND INTRODUCTION (2024)

Some things have changed since I wrote the above introduction. When I first released the drawing to the internet in 2020, I received three likes. After a bottle of rum, it finally occurred to me that wanting to do something on a grand scale was misplaced. We all view the world through a handheld screen on our phones and the 'Money' drawing is over a square meter in size. No one has the patience to figure something out before their thumb automatically clicks to the next image anyway. I then took photos of the big drawing and cut them into the individual elements but then the continuity of the overall idea suffered. So for the last two years, I have been taping the picture back together with poetry. I have written poems for most sections in an attempt to further your understanding of the drawing. I am not sure I have exceeded in this but It has been fun. I must warn you that I am not a trained poet or a "trained" artist but dedicated to trying to illustrate the problems that face continued life on what Bucky Fuller called 'Spaceship Earth' so a new operating manual may be written by us all.

I think we are now ready to begin our look at the 1%. Since a cartoon is an imaginary picture of reality we are free to start our journey any way we like. So, let's jump on one of the ships arriving at Seattle, Washington (upper left corner, upper left-hand panel). No need to bring a lot of clothes or even dress warmly. We won't be on board for long to keep our carbon footprint low.

SEATTLE, WASHINGTON

AND THE

GREAT NORTHWEST

This area was heavily forested at one time and during WWII it was considered a safe harbor because of its large size and the complexity of many islands and shoals as well as being the furthest harbor from both Germany and Japan. It was rather more important then than now. My father spent the war here developing sonar for submarines, while my mother and I lived with my grandmother in a house in the woods. I have been told that we never saw him during this period and my only memory is of the iceman and his horse-drawn cart. A big event for the under-five age group, getting free ice chips!

BIG JUNK

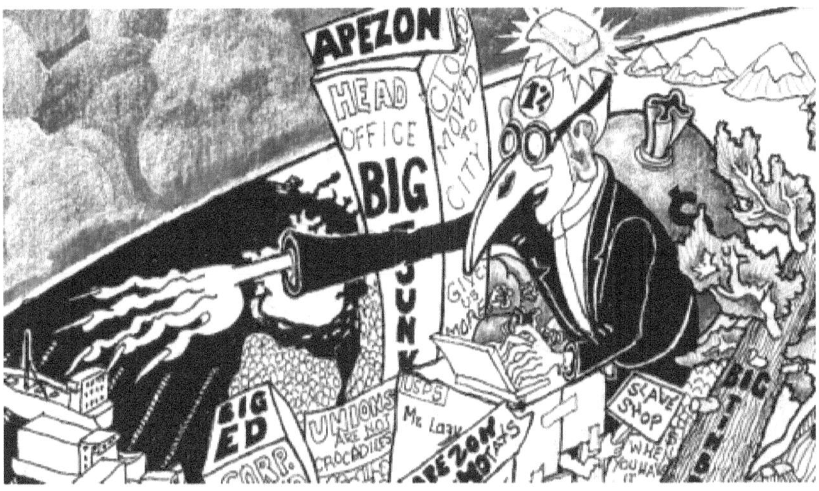

Washington state and Seattle can no longer be called the wonderland of 'rural America'. Some could argue that strip cutting was invented in Washington but I doubt that is true but, idyllic it no longer is. The shipbuilding of the past has been replaced by Big Pharm, Big Tech, and Big Junk because it is a gateway to and from Asia. As Big Money realized that Asia could make everything cheaper than here, in their own country, which then also opened new markets for lower-income people in these countries to buy their products as well, they flocked to little old Seattle the garden city of the West. The gardens are gone now and now Big Money is moving on.

Here is a poem I wrote in the 90s after my last visit to Washington. I suppose it sounds a bit nostalgic but I hope to use it to demonstrate some of what the whole country has lost in its shift to our new World Capitalism.

THE DRUG STORE

Wooden boardwalk covered by a shingled roof
It gave the old drugstore that Western look
Large windows with small panes
Lit shelves full of remedies for large pains
A long room with a wooden ceiling-high
Wood up and down and under, everything, lie
At the back, is where one paid
While in front, the doorbell played
On the left, the counter stretched
Where chrome, red-topped stools marched
To the sound of the Jute Box's blare
Eyes watch in the long mirror's, glare
Happy were the tunes and pretty was the waitress
Serving hamburgers and fries without stresses
Malts and shakes were much in demand
But, banana splits were always grand
Alcohol never, cokes were the fashion
This was the court of teenage passion
While in the store itself, all were free to wander
Among tables and shelves and hanging wonders
From bright patchwork quilts and lace curtains,
Cowboy saddles, and Stetson hats, found for certain
Only the teacups and carved chests were china-made
Not much else could be called, foreign aid
A pound of spuds, cherries, or berries was a "Nickel"
And two cents would buy you a 10-inch, "Dill" Pickle
In all of this, one could wonder at their leisure

Yes, it was our town's major feature
Then the war came and taught us about specialization.
Manufacturing and capitalization, all changed without realization
Of the loss of what we once had,
I think few are glad.
This drawing of course is not just about Drug Stores nor just about Washington State. It is in part, about a maga shift away from mom-and-pop stores to chain stores. The small business to the international chain store. What this represents is devastating to us all because it primarily drains capital from the masses and concentrates it on the few. When products of all types were made in many small firms and distributed through small stores to local populations this produced a balanced economy. In short, the small manufacturer employed local help. This local help became specialized in the skills needed to make the products and as the demand grew the workforce grew and the techniques necessary became more advanced. At the same time, transportation networks grew to supply local shops that were increasingly sold to a wider population. Millionaires were seldom made outside of the coal, steel, oil, and banking industry but the general population was employed.

As these individual companies grew, producing many different products, they invested heavily in finding ways to reduce their workforce by shifting to animation, as it is called. The machine-driven assembly line and the computer replaced huge numbers of accountants office staff and even workers with specific skills. Where once production was dependent on human skills it became dependent on machines and Artificial Intelligence and what followed was the Magna Corporation and a huge consolidation of wealth into a smaller and smaller group of individuals. By moving manufacturing to select poorer countries world markets have increased dramatically as in the case of China, Taiwan, Japan, and to some extent South Korea.

In less than 60 years the drug store where you could buy the best hamburgers with a dill pickle from the big wooden barrel in the corner and a malt or milkshake or share a banana split was gone. In its place the corporate coffee chain, the corporate hamburger chain, the pharmacy chain, the international travel agency, and now the online maga everything.

Since we are still in Washington State let's go over to Apezon. Now this is an interesting business. As I see it, it is more like a shadow or perhaps a bit of smoke. There is no Apezon to visit, it doesn't make anything but, it sells everything. Where does it get its products? From just about anywhere meaning mostly China. And it is at the moment, the largest retailer in the world, and its "owner" who is said to only own 13% of the business is heralded as the richest man in the world with the Covid 10 pandemic his wealth has been estimated at over a trillion dollars. The problem here is that we mere humans can't easily understand what a trillion is. Well, to begin with, you can't count that high so have a look at this chart:

One Thousand - 1,000

One Million - 1,000,000

One Billion - 1,000,000,000

One Trillion - 1,000,000,000,000

Just a lot of zeros? Try this; there are a Million seconds in 13 years, a Billion seconds in 31 years, and a Trillion seconds in 31,683 years. So, if we consider just the owner of Apezon, if he spent 1 Million dollars each hour of each of the 24 hours of a day it would take him 411 years to spend 1 Trillion dollars (statistics from Google). Getting the idea? Well, think about this. The Republican Senate and the newly elected president Donald Trump in 2017 gave a tax refund to the tune of 1-½ Trillion dollars most of which went to the 1% and it seems to be very questionable if the 1% even pay any taxes on their earnings. Percentage-wise, if they did, it would be less than the average worker's tax rate. I have read that online sales are not even taxable.

My 'Apezon' used to have its headquarters in Seattle but it fell out over the issue of taxation. The owner then came up with the wonderful idea of holding a competition where cities he thought would be more accommodating could submit what they would be willing to invest in public taxes to build Apezon a new headquarters in their city. During this period Apezon was creatively analyzed. It seems it employs a lot of people to run and maintain its computer system which is the very heart of its operation. It also needs a lot of people to put stickers on boxes. Everything else is mechanized. What you buy from Apezon sits in a basket which is picked up by a machine and set on an electronic trail that runs in the floor to an operator who watches the machine place the item in a box, drop in bubble wrap, close the box, and tape it shut, The operator then sticks the label on the box and the box then goes by conveyor belt to be machine loaded into a USP van. Each operator has 3 seconds to place the computerized sticker on the box.

APEZON

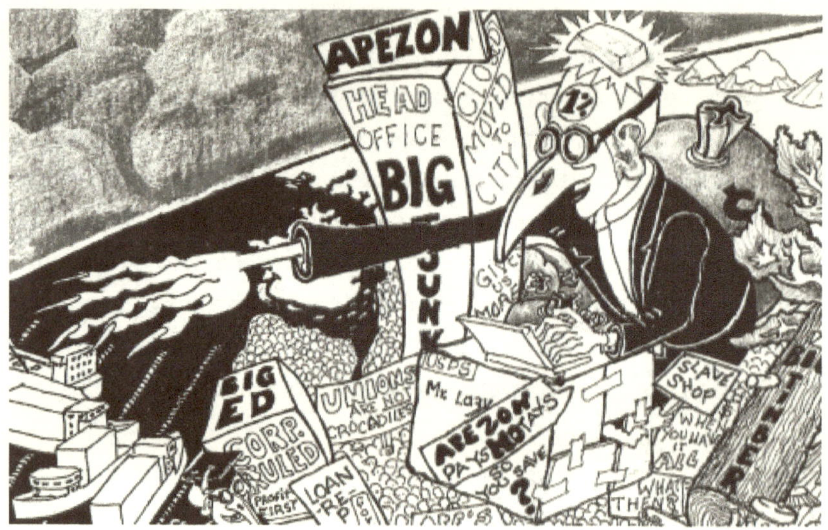

No alarm, every morning
I'm now my own man!
I get my credits, every month
My own room in the plan
I just ask the screen for my every want,
Apezon is always fair
Gone are those days of concentration
Physical labor, and chronic pain
Rushin to work with trepidation
Watching the mirror for Police to detain
Reading the "fake news" of the day
Apezon is the way
Now I live without all the fear
Of not working fast enough

In the hidden cameras lear
Being called to the office rebuff
Which can never be swayed
Apezon can never be delayed
No more hum of the stockroom
Robots on the floor, the wall,, the air, loom
They whine but, talk in the brume
All is in movement in windowless rooms
Adding speed to the zoom
Apezon is not doom
Pride, they said, was my contribution
And creates an excuse to not doubt
Will always be needed, in the confusion
Those who were happy to have built
But are no longer fulfilled
Apezon is always right
No problem can't be solved
With Artificial Intelligence all will be resolved
Facial Recognition in the Hands of the Police
Will make all of Society extremely Polite
Stay at home with safe delight
Apezon is your best friend
Society has few options to get what it wants
Built by many for the one who knows how profit works
Our leader is the richest, over a Trillion at last count
Money is everything, counted it to the smallest perks
All your problems he will surmount
Apezon is number one
What a genius.
To sell everything and anything online
Quick money to be made unhampered
No shops to maintain or displays to design

Few employees to handle or customers to pamper
Few workers to hire or benefits to scrimper
Apezon has it all
But we don't have to fear
With 75,000 Robots as slaves
And that is just for each year
$25,000,000 they plan to save
Apezon is never a place to shed a tear
Apezon is about profits
The future is here and it is now
No need to leave the house, Apezon is how
It is your bank, it is your shop
It is your food, it is your cop
Never again, the house will you have to pop
Apezon is god
Wait for just a minute
I must be a nut
What will happen to Apezon's disassociates?
And for all those that it terminates?
What will be their fate?
Don't we need a huge debate?
Do we need Apezon?

There have been many protests in this area. Some people are trying to save the old way of life and some are frustrated by the new. Apezon has been blamed for destroying that old institution, the bookstore, and many startups with brilliant ideas. They are accused of letting new ideas onto their platform until they are convinced it is a workable idea or product then they chase them off by upping their cut and then find someone to make the same thing. I am struck by the idea of what's to happen to all of us when the 1% sucks all the money out of the pond. AI and mechanization are here to do those jobs that haven't gone abroad. All of us can't hope to cook hamburgers in a vegan future. There is a lot to think about our future with Apezon as the model.

YOUR NATIONAL PARKS

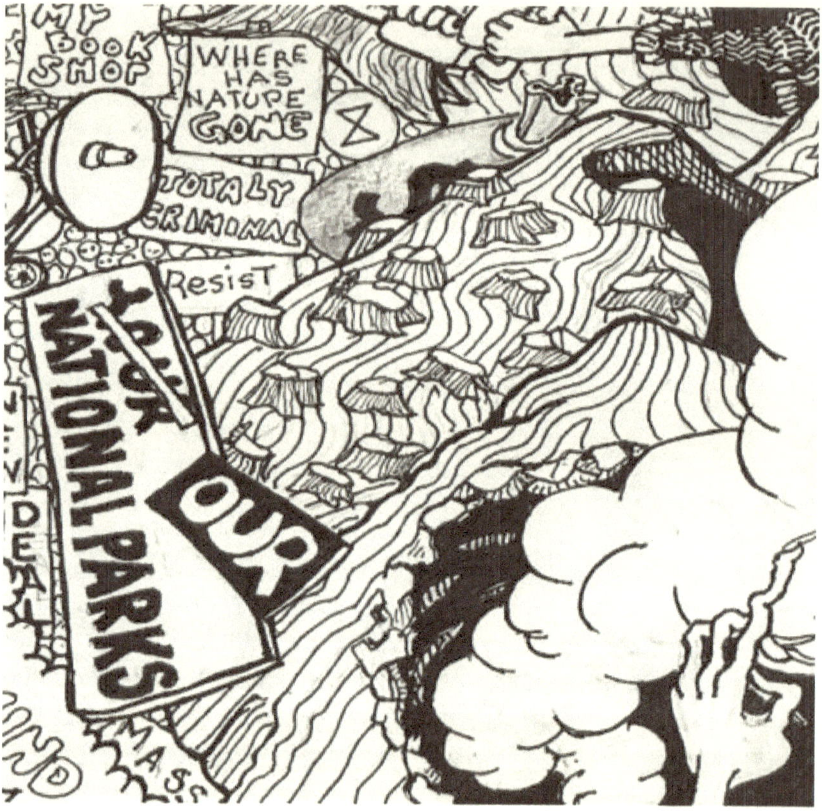

Let us walk over to have a look at YOUR NATIONAL PARKS, oops, they don't seem to be yours anymore. The government can now take money from whoever would like to give it to them and has seen fit to give concessions to big timber cutting, mining, and oil extraction to name a few paying interests. Am I exaggerating? I don't think so when you consider that less than 2% of the Old-growth Redwoods are left standing as an example. Wood is thought to be a "renewable"

18

resource except it is taken by "strip-cutting" large tracks of this national treasure. Strip-cutting takes all the branches, leaves, roots, and other spices out to create boards of glued composition. Forestry has become "Tree Farming" where the only interest is in how fast the next crop can be harvested. As we all know now, plants cooperate in forming communities of like interests that are called eco-systems. Strip-cutting destroys the community of plants and allows for forced-fed plantations laid out in rows for easy cheap maintenance. When wood of "quality" is needed just cut more old growth. The problem of course is what happens when all the old growth is gone?

In our many different Christian communities in the US much is said about how God prepared the world for us. No matter how much time you think it took him, her, or them to do it, the world was a very beautiful place when humans took the lead. The coastal Redwood of Northwest US was found throughout the world's temperate climate zones and wood was everywhere ready to service our first humans. Wood was not generally used to build shelters as in the US simply because it was not considered as substantial as earth and stone but was usually used for roof structures and floors and movable pieces. Most of the world's animals and birds were found in this huge covering and it is now said that the forest is essential to the balance of life on earth.

We haven't even come close to understanding the significance of what the tree means to our continued use of this earth for our survival. In the simplest terms, the tree takes carbon dioxide (CO_2) out of the air and converts it to oxygen while using the carbon to grow. We inhale 'free' oxygen while exhaling excess carbon back into the air as CO_2 but we can't take the oxygen from the carbon without the help of the tree to separate them. These oxygen 'pumps' were once everywhere and are now being destroyed to make...money. Money does not make oxygen nor is it being used for anything of this nature. National Parks were created to protect these trees as a national treasure for everyone to enjoy while conserving their much-needed service. Who can say that the US National Parks are not some of the most beautiful places on earth?

20   STEVEN SELBY

the US National Parks are not some of the most beautiful places on earth?

BIG TIMBER

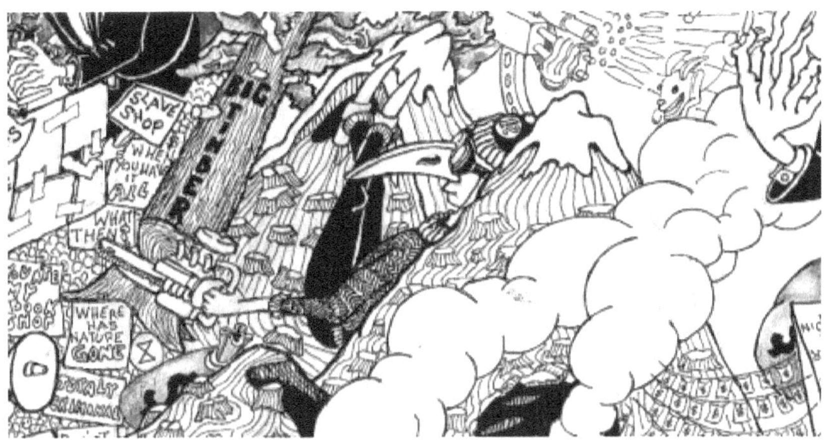

Dark and damp the rays of the sun, lightly
Dance around dripping branches lit brightly
Giants of centuries past once shaded dinosaurs
Now entwine their branches along Pacific shores
Mountains High kiss the cloudy air
Wearing thick coats of green and fair
Dense and lonely groves should not be feared
For they are just the locks of God's living beard
You may have thought that trees were good for not
Pretty to please, sweet to smell, but prone to rot
Ah, but this is not the case! From Little Honey Bee
To Grizzlies, the flowers and fruits, provide much glee
Where once trees spread their Boroughs across all lands
Their beauty now rests in the government's hands
Safe they should be, you may have thought
But, the awful truth is they are not!
What is beautiful is not being left to rot
But, something dreadful is happening to the whole lot
What then is that sound that rattles the flourishing forest tall

It is the folly of foolish fiends, chainsaw madness falling them ALL
But, why, you may ask, do you not know that greed is rife
Money, money, money is the bitter honey of life
Why take just one? Take the whole damn lot. Strip-cut it clean
Your National Parks are THEIRS! Big Timber has a dream
Then, why is it that we can't plant more? We could but, the government
Deplores that which is best, if it interferes with their enrichment
Together we could replant all those wonderful trees called, timber
We just have to vote together for what matters. Please, Remember!

BIG MINE

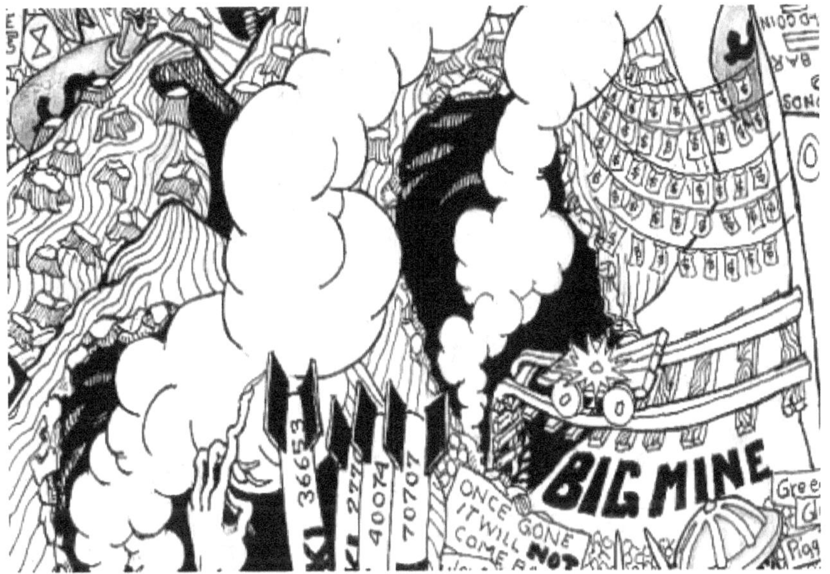

Mining is a huge issue that deserves to be taken very seriously. The Earth is a finite object, by this I mean the resources that we have here on Earth are gone once they are used. In a few cases, they could be recycled but at the present, usually are not. The prevailing attitude is to take it as cheaply as you can and when it has served its purpose, through it away. Where that should be is a question no one seems to be interested in. An example is the by-product of atomic energy. What is the plan for the lithium that is now being used in batteries? What happens to senseless plastic? If there is a toxic by–product, where does that go? The Ocean? Mining has continually demonstrated that it takes then leaves it to the devil to clean up. But, the big question is what happens when a much-needed resource is used up or no longer obtainable? It is on this issue that we are running wild. All of the world powers are using our

taxes for a new era of space exploration. Permanent platforms in space so they can see if the moon, asteroids, Mars, or other planets have anything useful. In the meantime trash the planet and extract what they can.
Is it mine,
is it yours,

    it is ours
    This is the question!

Ah, but,
There are others

    Money loudly speaks
    And, Gets what it seeks

He has money
We had some

    Who controls
    What is done

We elect the controllers
We pay them some

    He pays them
    A lot more

The controllers, give him rights
He extracts the resource

    We pay what
    We are force

He becomes Richer

We become poorer
The resource is lost
Forever

Now, the Earth is Scared
It no longer

Has our needs
He becomes the controller

He says, take it all
We say no, this must end

Now the Earth
Has changed

Fallow Water, Lost Forrest
Dead Soil, Polluted Air

Toxic Waste,
Empty Seas

He says, More!
We say Stop!

The Earth says
There is Little time left

Global Depletion and
Global Warming are

Not a game
IT MUST BE SHAMED

Nothing will last forever

Use what is left

    With CARE
    We must BEWARE!

HUNTING

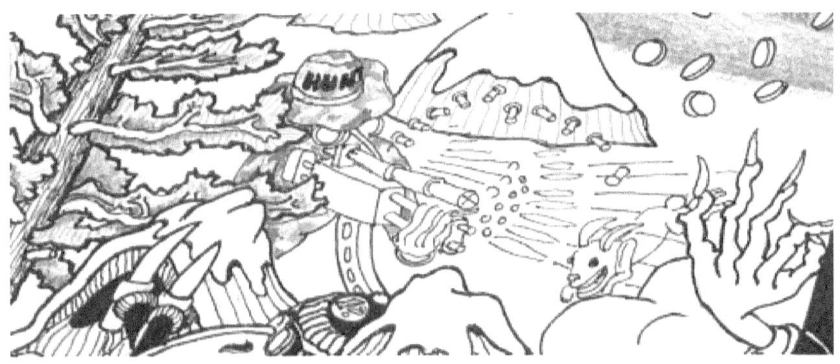

If the butterfly or beetle bathes in the light
Their brilliant colors flash and delight
Why are these things killed so quickly?
With a dab of Round-up for them to lick?
xxx
Birds in pairs or flocks,
Sweeping around the treetops
Dancing among the vegetable beds
Must they all be made dead?
XXX
That mole in the ground
Can't even see a hound
Or even make a sound
Is best in a trap, to be found?
XXX
That small bushy tail
Makes a rabbit hard to trail
So a trap with a flap

Is more apt to zap?
XXX
The fox is fast
And can last
So why is it best to be made to chase
Before the hounds make waste?
XXX
Now the deer is not to fear
But it nibbles everything near
The best defense is a fence
Not to be made a feast.
XXX
The elk only eats grass
But the hunter can't let it pass
s it best to take it with an elephant gun
And then collect dust where it is hung?
XXX
The Grizzly bear gives such a fright
Most hunters would rather take flight
But soon we will have a drone
That will kill them from home.
XXX
Now the cougars are elusive
Known to eat hunters, though reclusive
Do not need the Second Amendment
Armed with teeth that are not adornment
XXX
The bison was decimated before a gun
Was so much fun!
Now we could kill millions
With the guns, we use to kill humans?
XXX

Speaking of which, why is it so many die
More frequently than eating apple pie?
What is this crazy need to kill?
Wouldn't it be better to just chill?
XXX
Has human nature gone to hell?
Or is this all some sort of bell,
Marking our entrance to an unthinkable Apocalyptic life, that is avoidable?
XXX
Why kill?
In love Is there no thrill?
Or are we all to violence and must fall?
And then stuffed to hang on the wall?
XXX
Now, if this is not right
We must enter the fight
Not with each other
But, to make this better

It is said that mankind was once hunter-gatherers' and this justifies hunting in this day and age of supermarkets and home delivery. This is not an issue directly involving the 1% but BIG GUNS is selling a product that is used in hunting animals in the wild. On the one hand, we have battery production of animals in restricted conditions using hormones and bleach to counter the toxic effects of this type of BIG FARMING, and on the other hand, BIG PHARM, producing chemicals to kill insects and 'weeds'. These norms are having a devastating effect on animals throughout the world. I don't think it is out of place here to have a rethink on how hunting fits into a new way of thinking in our modern world.

BIG BANKING

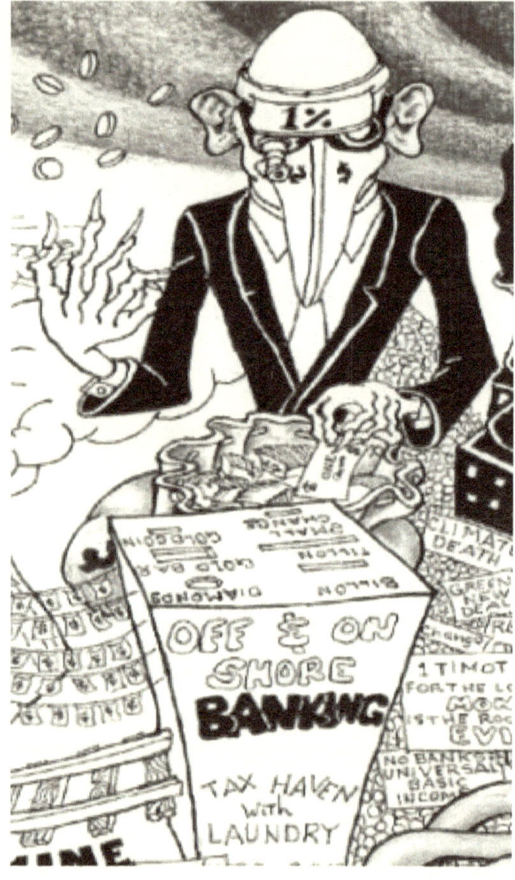

Fortunes are hidden in far-off reaches
With blue skies and sandy beaches
OOO
Mighty banks with Wall Streets help
Hide their Money next to kelp
OOO
One-percenters and Loan Sharks' riches
Find their way to coral sand nitches
OOO
Were global banks hide their money
Is not next to bees and honey
OOO
Why the fuss to hide their wealth
They simply don't what National Health
OOO
Your taxes make them fatter
While their money builds towers that flatter
OOO
Is it wise to be surprised
At what their Money buys
OOO
That little bank beneath the palms
May have bought heaps of bombs
OOO
Dictators flourish in the sun and shade
And who knows who a bank may aid
OOO
Because it is all discreetly hidden
Somewhere well below heaven
OOO
We must ask about the facts
Why banks aren't responsible for their acts

OOO
Could it be that with their untold powers
That they are taking what is ours
OOO
It's a sorry state when the money they take
are a raft on the lake of their own mistakes
OOO
Will that money buy something favorable?
Like public officials who are available
OOO
Are our Congressional controllers
Just the bank's high rollers
OOO
Was there ever a banker jailed
For indiscretions hailed?
OOO
Or was his yacht bought?
From our savings hard fought
OOO
Now resting in the breeze
Behind the reef in Belize
OOO
If you are just a little guy
And your bank account is very shy
OOO
Why is it that your bank has no offices?
Is "online" some sort of metamorphosis?
OOO
If money is no longer on paper,
How is a bank your helper?
OOO
If you give a bank your hard-earned

It loans it to another un-observed
OOO
Why then do we have to pay to play
Has the system gone astray?
OOO
If the rich can hide their wealth offshore
Why do I need a credit score?
OOO
It is rather intriguing that, "my vote counts"
But, wealth owns Congress, not counted
OOO
As a Government for the wealthy,
By the wealthy. That leaves 1% healthy.
OOO
Where they hide it, is not important,
That they get away with it, is abhorrent.
OOO
Yes, banks play the numbers game
And they will never be tamed
OOO
Until Money is not to be gained
And humanity is reframed
OOO
Would money be the root of all evil,
If it worked for the good of all people?
OOO
Nope, not possible, never happen,
Much simpler to be told what to do

BIG AGRO

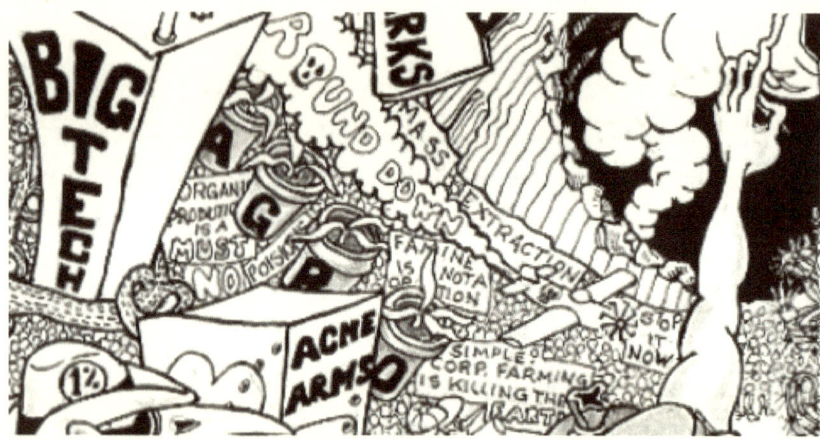

How did Big Agro get it so wrong
Perhaps they listened to Big Pharm's song
Everything is just chemicals, what a con
OXO
"Splash a little water, deserts will grow"
"Throw chemicals in the hole, where you sow"
"Our GM seeds resist our weed Killer wherever it might blow"
OXO
Killing the planet is what it is doing
At best, farming is trying,
This type of farming is about dying
OXO
It is easy to ask the question
If the earth can function
For thousands of years without intervention
OXO

Why do we now need
Chemical companies who don't heed
The simple fact that all that grows, is not a weed
OXO
In a system so precious
We should all be conscientious
That life is an illustrious Interdependencies
OXO
If mankind was not so interested in money
We would be able to appreciate life's great harmony
And thus immerse ourselves in the earth symbiotically
OXO
Rather than seeing ourselves as having been given the earth
As a playground to use and abuse like money's in church
We could all be part of the sphere of life's great worth
OXO
Ecological is a word and not a solution
But, understanding it could give us a system to help our evolution
Which would help us reverse our pollution
OXO
It is not very difficult to be one's self in the forest
Or around plants and flowers, one doesn't have to be a florist
To feel the connection we all have to all the life it fosters
OXO
Billionaires have a lot of money
But, they don't make honey
And there is nothing about them remotely funny
OXO
Agriculture must become the way we all feel
Centered on a thought, like, A New Green Deal
Before, the safety of the planet could become real
OXO

Throwing aid to a chemical farm
Is just doing the world extreme harm
It is not the earth but the system, we need to reform
OXO
What might it be like, if the earth were a goddess
That we loved and delighted, at all that she begot us
Would money still dominate us?
OXO
Apart from the food that goes to feed us,
The materials that we use to house us;
And all the air we need to enrich us
OXO
She has built a world of Botany, Mineralogy, and Zoology to, enlighten
us
With endless arrangements of clouds, lighting, and sunsets, to delight
us
Manifest variations of colors, and forms, to entertain us
OXO
And thrown in our emotions, and a mind, that will guide us, if we let it
Without which we might be duped into thinking, money, is important
bit
But in reality, money is messing us up and we need, to omit it,
OXO
I suggest that the Big Agro must take on a new form, we live for
Not that nature should run wild but, we use nature and its force
That we do not forget, natural harmony and balance are the way forth.
OXO
We need not tame nature, but rather, study how to put it to better use
The exploration of space should parallel the exploration of soil, even if
it seems abstruse,
And use the knowledge that the greening of the earth is fundamental,
there can be no abuse

BIG ED

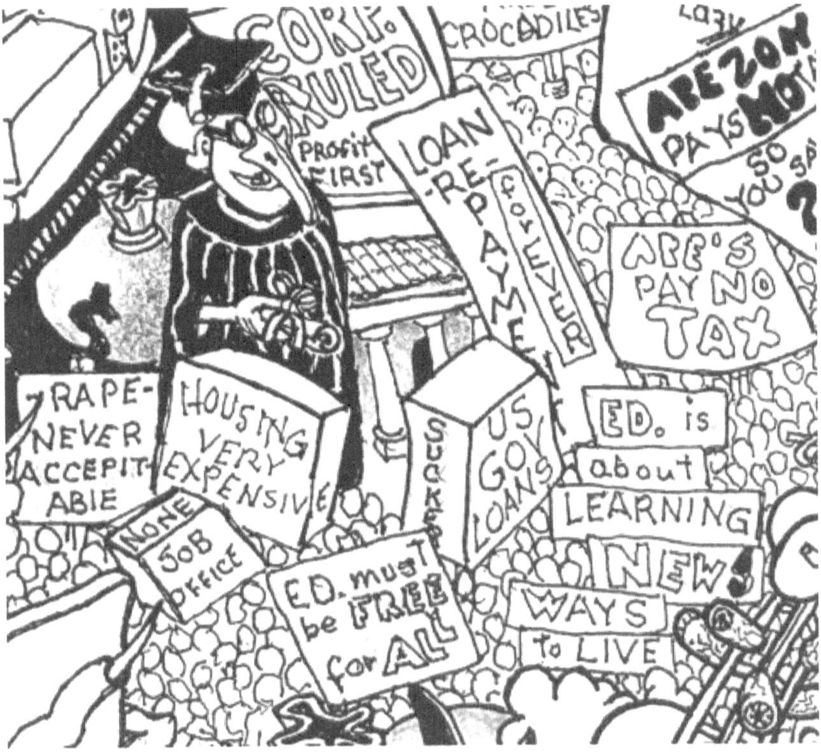

If you think education is just for city folk

That's is not a very reasonable joke

Best, we all advance, even the cow poke

XOX

We all start life in our bodily shell

Windows must open so we dwell

In a heaven of understanding, not a Hell

XOX

The three Rs have there place

As does roaming around cyberspace
But there is much more to embrace
XOX
Tolerance is a worthy grace
Often we are forced to face
That what we don't want to take place
XOX
We live on a rock in outer space
With billions of others to interface
Each in his separate headspace
XOX
We should all know that decisions
Will encompass many collisions
Then, education by definition
XOX
Is a social resolution of the majority
On the norms in life that have superiority
With the guidance of acceptable authority
XOX
Let me cut to the chase
Education is the base
Of how we go face-to-face
XOX
We have made schools
As the basic tools
To keep us from being fools
XOX
All deserve this opportunity
To protect our world community
From disunity from importunity

BIG TECH

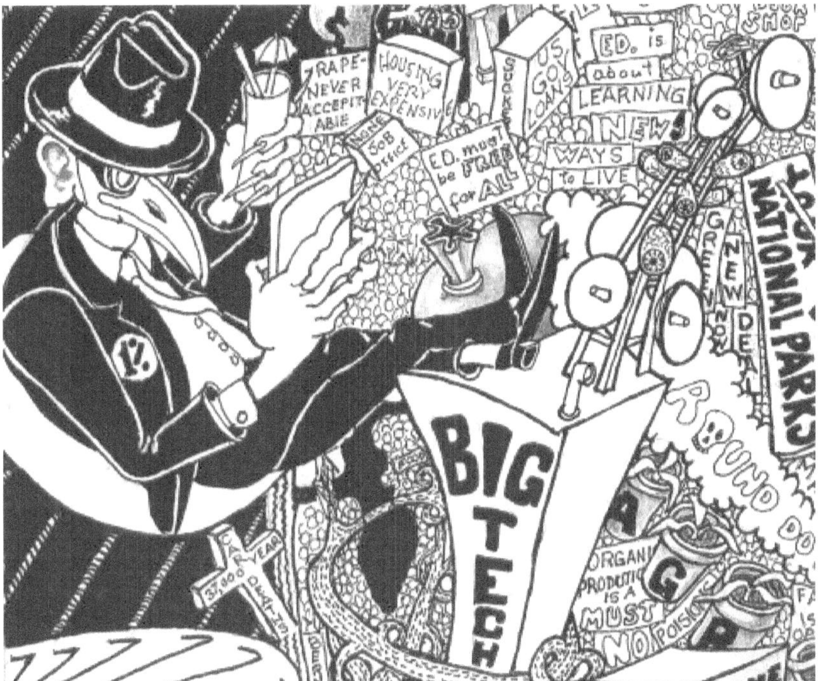

Big Technology has changed the World and the way that we live in it. This huge change has everything to do with my drawing, "money, Money, MONEY", and the creation of this book. It is not that all of these changes are bad but the impact of the technological changes that are taking place seem to be controlled by chance rather than detailed consideration. The big Tech companies have produced an unprecedented change in the balance of wealth and created a superclass of the wealthy. Super wealth unfortunately does not bestow super powers of insight, compassion, and leadership demonstrating the need for a new rethink on how we organize society.

Here are some quotes from Bukky Fuller's thoughts on reorganizing society, "You never change things by fighting the existing reality. To change something build a new model that makes the existing model obsolete" and "You can make money or you can make sense. The two are mutually exclusive, Humanity is acquiring all the right technology for all the wrong reasons.

Here is my suggestions;

With the birth of the internet

So much positive information we could be gleanning

Except for lies and deceits from the fiendish set

And the trolls and the bots constant threatening

What a handy device the smartphone

Not just portable but sounds so charming in church

There has never been an equal to this philosopher's stone

It provides such sound heart-warming smirch

All those centuries wasted searching for gold

It is right here wrapped in bright plastic

For only a few has it brought wealth untold

But its value is very elastic

For the rest, it makes no sense

By not providing real human communication

Of a tool that could brighten commonsense

It is frantically fueling rapid negation

Perhaps the new technology should be combined with an old theology. Remember when the earth had a mother? 'Mother Nature' she was called and very respected for her beauty and charm. She had moments of violence and caused suffering in her anger but she was our mother and respected for the bounty of food sand materials she provided. And we were not alone then because she had provided us with animals, birds, and fish of all sorts that roamed the earth and sea with us. Forests reached from coast to coast and the climate was predictable. But that all started to fail as the car brought forward oil and mining on a large scale.

With it came Big Money, bigger and bigger Corporations, Big Tech, and war. As pointed out by Fuller, "All the right technologies for all the wrong reasons". They can't be the right reasons if the accumulation of money is the driving force in society. That makes no sense. There can be no other reason for mankind to be here if it doesn't include the protection of Mother Nature and her ecology which is the very thing that makes the existence of humanity possible here.

How can Big Tech be responsible for this? Big Tech, Big Oil, and all the other Big's are made up of people with ideas and abilities who work together mainly to find improvements to our lives, as they should be doing. But, this system is ruled by capitalism where groups or individuals who have money pay for the 'work' of many individuals with the expectation that their money will bring greater financial rewards for their investments. The inverters expect to control the direction, the use, and the rewards that the company obtains. In most cases, the object of the total enterprise is the creation of money for the few who already have it.

Money has become the religion or at least the driving force of humanity. Each must work to get the basics for their existence while a few accumulate more and more until the balance has moved toward slavery. We are making all the right technologies for all the wrong reasons.

The Earth may have more people than it can support at present but the issue is that for space ship earth to continue on its journey with humanity on board, we must recognize that our major responsibility is to the ship and its crew which includes every last one of us and to do that, the ecology of the planet and the security of its crew must be our focus. The present model is dead wrong and needs to be changed. If you are expecting me to provide the solution at this point, I can't! But, I do believe that it is time that we get involved in looking for a New model. Division and rancor are so much of the human experience because we have such a hard time seeing past our noses we must endeavor to find a new way forward.

The technology is available for the goal of reducing our past and present bad effects on the planet. Big Money has had a big part to play in creating our current model. It needs to have an even bigger part in changing how we live more positively or it must go. We can not have a model where AI is developed to make human beings redundant. Who in the hell needs robots? We need above all good farming methods, adequate health services, free education, a belief in each other, and an endless supply of courage.

BIG ARMS

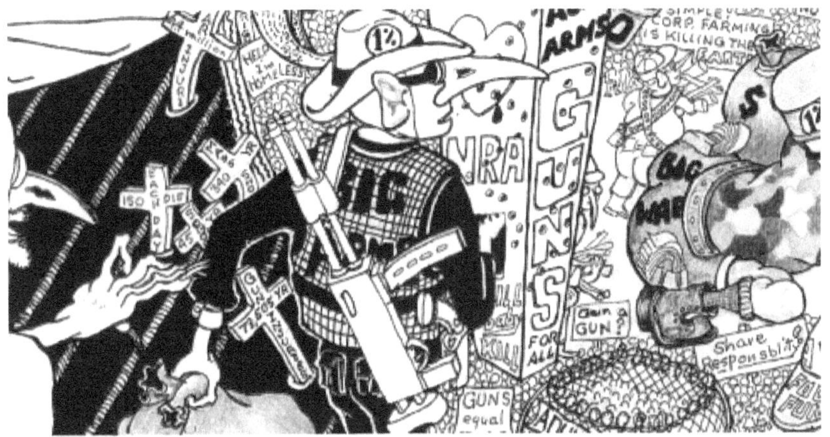

If Johnny's Big Arms are used to harm
That is clearly, an offense
But, friends of Johnny sound the alarm
Saying, "It is his defense".
-O-
If Johnny didn't have 'Big Arms'
He couldn't have caused the offense
But, his friends say it's his right
To have this much-needed defense"
-O-
Now the National Rifle Ass.
Tell us that the constitution
Gives us all the right to have Big Arms
And that is all we need for conformation
-O-
The Constitution, in a small mention
Big Arms are acceptable

When there is a need for a militia
To make the nation resistible
-O-
From, the people who make Big Arms,
We hear very little
Which fills us with alarm
Is this some sort of fiddle
-O-
Not at all, they are just shy
They would sell a gun
To anyone who would buy
Ask no questions, just watch the fun
-O-
It is simply in their interest
To sell, what this hell
If they be anarchist or fascist
What is the difference? They make money, swell
-O-
If you think this is not the case
Then why are there so few background check laws
Could it be that in Government is their base
Senators who receive campaign help, that is their fall
-O-
But, the biggest problem with Big Arms
Is that everyone has a goddamn gun
You would expect there to be one hell of an Alarm
Because getting shot is not all that much fun
-O-
You could even say it is deadly
Might call it a Pandemic
Or, it is even unfriendly
Just chronic

-O-
Is this the Wild West?
People, please, stop the guns
Grow up! No killing is best
Might try chewing bubble gums!
-O-
The gun issue is very much an issue along Party political philosophies. The Democrats endorse the working class and support social improvement that they feel democracy supports. In the case of gun ownership they except that the population has the right to own guns mainly for protection in the home. Military arms specifically made for the killing of other humans and weapons that are assembled from parts that can not be identified have no place in society. Guns for hunting are acceptable if used for that reason and follow laws in the control of hunting. The Democratic party feels that military-style guns that are continually used for mass shootings must be banned.

The Grand Old Party (Republican Party) that is credited with banning slavery is supportive of everyone having as many guns and ammunition as they want. It is no secret that manufacturers of guns support this party heavily. The GOP has opposed gun restrictions of any type and has demonstrated the desire to reinterpret the laws of US democracy. They have been accused of advocating for an insurrection to the constitution. As I write this Donald Trump is the de facto leader of this party and rerunning for the presidency of the US. Guns may have an unspoken future use for this party. God help us.

◆

BIG OIL

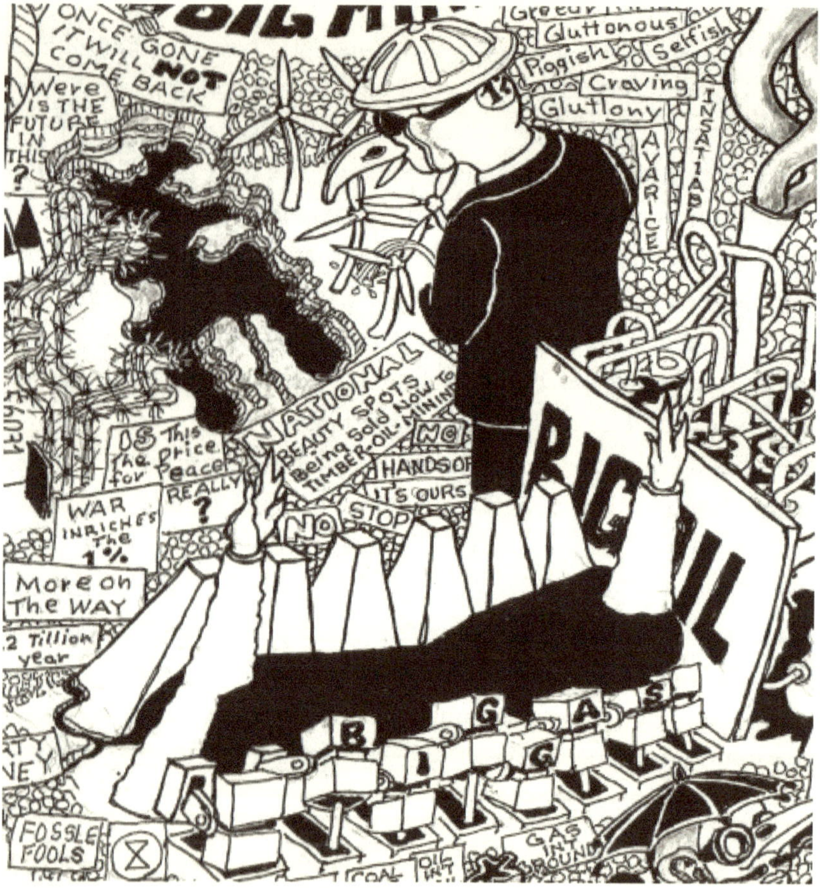

Big Oil is a big story that needs to be told.

Even though it's not that old. Let us begin with changes, bold.

Mankind had just the horse until steam was harnessed which had more force

But steam required fire and a lot of wood to source.

-X-

The internal whats-it motor took forever
Many different men endeavored, to find something clever
That would propel a chariot that would carry you to the next space
The one that won was based on what now has to be replaced.

-X-

That black gooey stuff that Texas floats upon
Became the fuel that cars depended on, but at this point, that was way beyond
This little motor might do the trick, but the horse was still not licked
How could you stay on course without a steed was the trick

-X-

In the beginning, the wagon with a motor was a bust
Then Henry came along with an idea robust, totally nonplussed
He wanted to assemble his little gadget in a way no one could envision
The "assembly line" would help change the world's horizon.

-X-

What, sitting in a line making something very fine?
Not quite, but, his model 'T' line, will always be the light of that time.
A" bucket" for two, with a floor and a door,
Fenders are connected by a "running" board.

-X-

A windshield to keep the bugs out of your teeth
A foldable weather sheath, and not much underneath
It had two speeds forward to traverse and went up hills in reverse
Gave the world an affordable car and a lot of entrepreneurs.

-X-

How could we have known
That Ford gave us an ominous omen, that his idea would be our tombstone
"You can have any color you want, as long as it is Black!"
He once said, and to this, I will come back

-x-

This man was not a hack,
More a visionary on the wrong track, but it was humanity that got distracted.
Enraptured, they manufactured machines with no thought of them being destructive
They just jumped in, not knowing how to swim, they just wanted to be productive.

-x-

About this time there just happened to be a war
What better time to explore, new machines that contribute to the gore
In war, a lot of things happen and discoveries heighten
And go into making this a boom, for all of mankind wanted to frighten.

-x-

And boy, zoom they sure did!
New roads and bridges and ditches made the whole country prodigious
Collaborating in mankind's elevation, the government even guided us
Cars gave men the illusions of religion, they had become prestigious

-x-

And then came another war to intervene
This one, was a war for the machine, and almost all of them ate gallons of gasoline
The forces needed resources and Big Oil was formed to find these sources
As these war machines evolved, the problem of where to find gas was solved

-x-

Crude oil was found almost everywhere
After the war, machines made transport flared, humanity could go anywhere

More motors, more materials, more bridges, and more ditches, all made more riches
Riches are made if someone else pays and oil companies found all the ways.

-x-

And then the rich bitches bought politicians
Who presented propositions, to increase their ambitions through shenanigans?
Leaving the taxpayer responsible, while they avoid all taxes or repercussions.
And took a lot of government handouts that made them kings of dissimulations.

-x-

So, what's the other problem?
Car, there are over a billion of them, and this is just a quantum
Because each motor turns oxygen into carbon dioxide, we may soon all die.
The energy we are using has a cost, and it is we who will be saying goodbye.

-x-

That is of course,
If the car doesn't drive us back to the horse, or traffic doesn't twist us into a noose
Man's single most dangerous object, more than those used in the horrors of wars
Metal boxes, coffins of traffic, spewing pollutants, black is the true color of cars.

-x-

Don't laugh, it is not funny, and hard to bear!
Cars have been around for a hundred years, and all bring smog with a tear

Orange sunsets and wildfires are almost an everyday occurrence to admire
Add bigger and more hurricanes, tornados, and storms, and soon we will expire.

-x-

It's happening folks
I'm not going to beat the drums and sell you, hell, but it is time you woke
I'll just ask, why does it have to be this pathway, always about pay?
Global warming is not the smart way, we need to be brave and find a better way.

-x-

We now have renewable energy
BIG OIL could be obsolete. No more oil spills, pipelines broken, or treachery.
No oil-based plastics, sprays that kill, or chemical substitutes that grow bland food
Maybe, we will even wake up to the fact that Ford's car should not be our main tool!

-x-

Do you think the future could bring
Mass transport trains and trolleys that ring, and big ships with those sail-like things,
Or Cities that are like parks where everywhere there are trees and plants,
And manufacturing that is owned by all, providing health and grants?

-x-

Is this totally crazy?
No borders to cross, the freedom to work and live and keep busy
Corporations are replaced by cooperation, not a life of work that maintains poverty

A belief in the sustainability of Mother Earth that teaches lives of
poetry.

-x-

Is my madness complete?
No more wars to massage the cruelty of the elite, defeat of the deceit of
Wall Street
No more kings, dictators, or billionaires, just human order as needed
for survival
A new world where humanity rejoins the beauty and pageantry of
Gaia's revival.

-x-

The car was a dream gone bad
Not all dreams need to end sad
But we must understand
Dreams can also make us glad

-x-

The earth is the biggest dream of them all
Let us not let it fall
It is we who will fail
Unless a new, we set sail

-x-

Big Oil is gone
It never belonged
Something new should be our song
Sung to nature's throng

-x-

With Giai as a guide
Cultivate what is good
For she gives without debt
With returns on every bet.

BIG CRIME

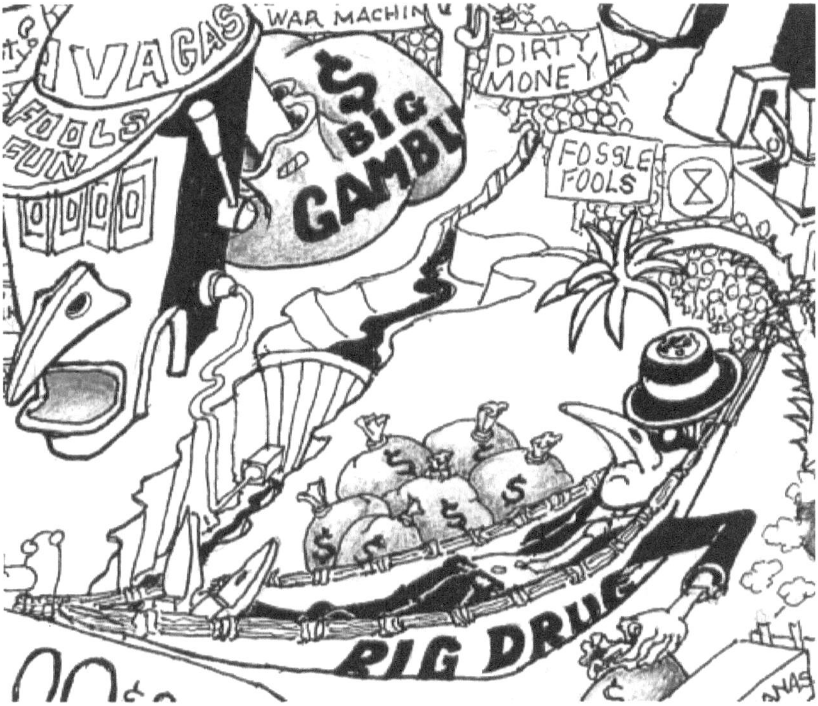

Is it Lui doing a heist with Luigi driving
Or the homeless lady who stole food 3 times, now doing life
The kids smoking pot which is thriving
Do we count all those guys who beat their wives
Now where is all this crime merging
Are we sure we could use more police intangling
xoxo
Gamblig can be a drug as taking drugs is a gamble
Both may be pervented or rehabilitated by education
Rather than by a continual political grumble

Developing lives that fosters understanding and foundation
A society organized around a collective goal
Surely is going to create a life more whole
xoxo
But, maybe we are looking in the wrong direction
If only one percent has the same wealth
As 60% of the total population
We might want to look at what goes on beneath
The endless struggle to exist
In that way, we might find the crime, to resist
xoxo
Before we start we want to know
Just what is a crime," An unlawful act"
Which is a bit, of a blow
Because it doesn't tell us all the facts
Like who it is that makes the law
And what morality is it that could have a flaw
xoxo
Around morality, tender steps we must take without fault
Like all mankind, the best soup is what 'they' make
While all the others need more salt
But, morality is not fake, in it, we all have a stake
I say morality must suit the whole
And should be defined as not falling in the hole
xoxo
So, I ask why is it that so, so many have so little
While just a very few have way way more
Is there some sort of fiddle in this riddle?
Is it moral, that the whole should be so poor?
This is not being civil
This is just being med-evil
xoxo

<u>All endeavors</u> need help! This would imply
No matter how hard we try
That many must help to supply
Every little thing we buy
Which makes any product
A community project
xoxo

<u>Then a</u> crime must occur
When a company is worth 1 trillion
While the workers are not secure
And have to ask the government for added provisions
Oh, this is just called Capitalitalistic
It is a normal characteristic
xoxo

<u>Yet another</u> offense is when Senators pass
A law that permits them to except
Dark money from any corporate sass
Regardless of what the donner expects
And this happens apparently without a second thought
Everyone in government is bought
xoxo

<u>So those</u> that are supposed to represent the many
Obligate themselves to the few who are rich
Who not only don't pay their taxes, not any!
And just love these big 'taxpayer' handouts, which
Means that they want to cut money for the needy
To cover free money for the greedy
xoxo

<u>If this</u> isn't a crime against humanity
Then what morals should we display?
A world crawling with human poverty
At the whim of the fat and greedy who disobey

Or a world of sharing and respect
Built on a communal aspect
Xoxo
<u>We can</u> all see that the system is open to corruption
And that dictators come in many different clothes
Even if dressed in total reduction
The 60% must stand together to oppose
The power that money, in the hands of a few
It will not be used in turning the final screw
xoxo
<u>Liberty</u> is sweet and should never be cheated
Lincoln gave us all equality
And Uncle Sam's obligation to all, to not be defeated
In rendering our rights without apology
Representation of the majority is the sole obligation
Congress and money are not part of that preservation

BIG PRISON

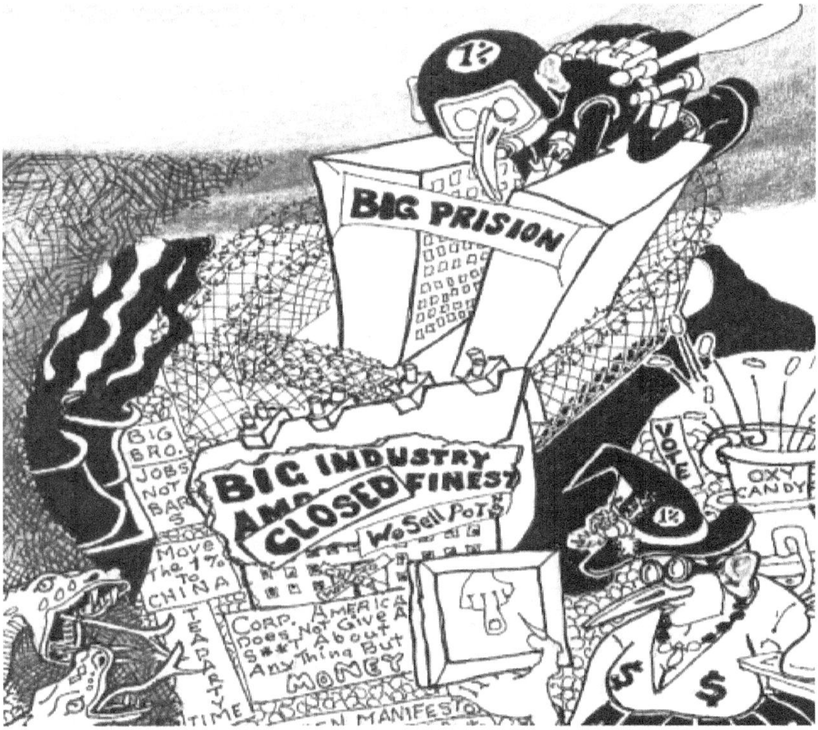

The Slammer, where one goes if they don't follow the rules
Fair enough, really, otherwise more would act like fools
|||||

Responsibility, is a keyword in any system of Government
The bigger question, is who enforces this empowerment
|||||

To follow the rules, democracy creates a group of scholars
Who oversee a panel of equals, that judge the dodgers
|||||

Those who fail the test of this system become, the guests of the State
Where once the state-supervised, now those judged are Big Money's
inmate
lllll
Still, at the state expense, one might expect curtains and potted plants
Ah, but, to make poets, is not in big money's plannings
lllll
Something with a larger profit portfolio in mind
Surely someone doing time must find a way to use their time.
lllll
Now work is so much fun and with the best profits in the short run
Well, roll up your sleeves, this is not going to be a dry-run
lllll
But, where are all those billionaires that the system snagged?
There is not a single one to be found here, that was bagged
lllll
Why is it that if you have millions of dollars you can't have fun
In the Joint with the others and make money for your chums?
lllll
Shouldn't any just system. support equality, before the law?
Then, where are all those bankers, who to the law, said blah?
lllll
Bailed out by public money but denied a rest of duration,
To wear prison fashions, and help support the system's intention
lllll
Million and Billionaires face so much unfairness and loneliness
It must be addressed with a return of equality, justice, and trustfulness

BIG WAR

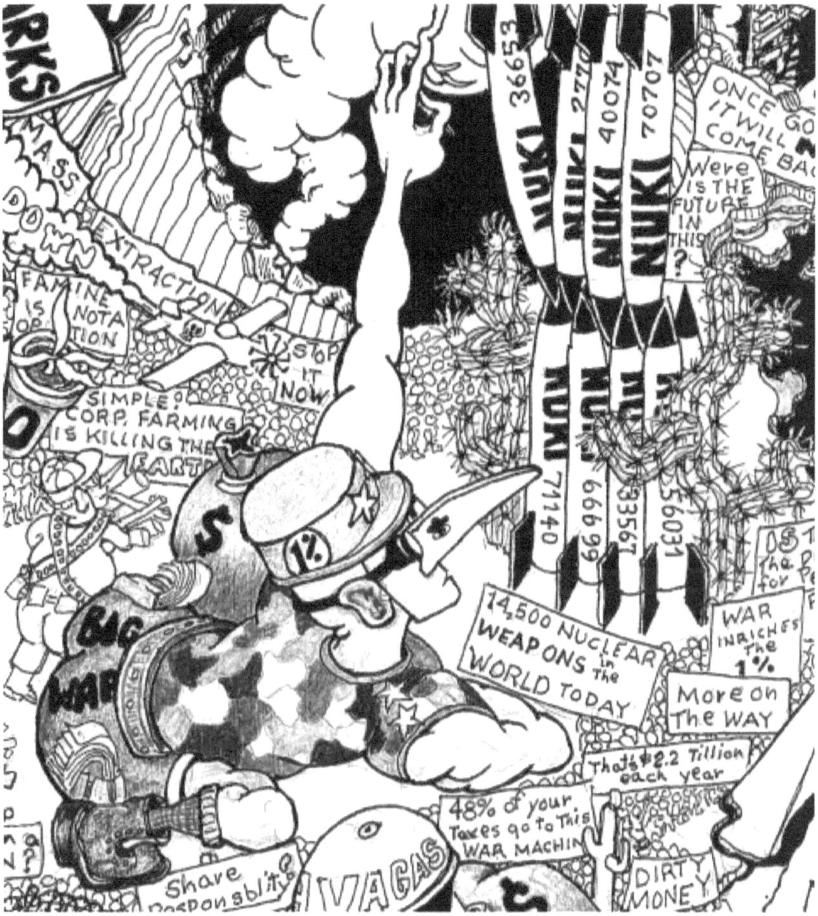

While spending most of our taxes on machines of war
I'm not very clear on how we can clamor for peace
To the world's community of political beasts
It must just sound like some useless lore,
pbpb

Always willing to back our friends, allows
Big War to continually rotate its stock
It should never come as a great shock
That money sees no need to cover its vows
pbpb
As the stockpile grows Big War needs to show
Its determination to provide weapons of peace
So all that money will never cease
No matter how the political wind might blow
pbpb
When the wars against war are slow
What is the difference if the old stuff
Is passed on to the police to help snuff
Any local disagreement that might grow
pbpb
You may see this is a problem when you arm
The total population with tactical weapons of offense
And tell them that is solely for their defense
They are very likely to shoot anything perceived to harm.
pbpb
Still, you don't have to worry very much about
Tactical Nuclear Weapons being given to the police lot
The Army will surely step in to stop any rebellion that ought
To slow down the movement of any money that may sprout
pbpb
I do wonder, if we could turn Battleshapes into gardens
Or airplanes into housing for the unfortunate
They both would need extensive modifications
But for the problem of pest control they have plenty of armament
pbpb
But what should we do with all of our old warheads?
I suppose it would be easy to sell them in a flea market

Or perhaps they could be used for digging flower beds
Somewhere In the Valley of the Dead, on the moon

BIG MED AND INSURANCE

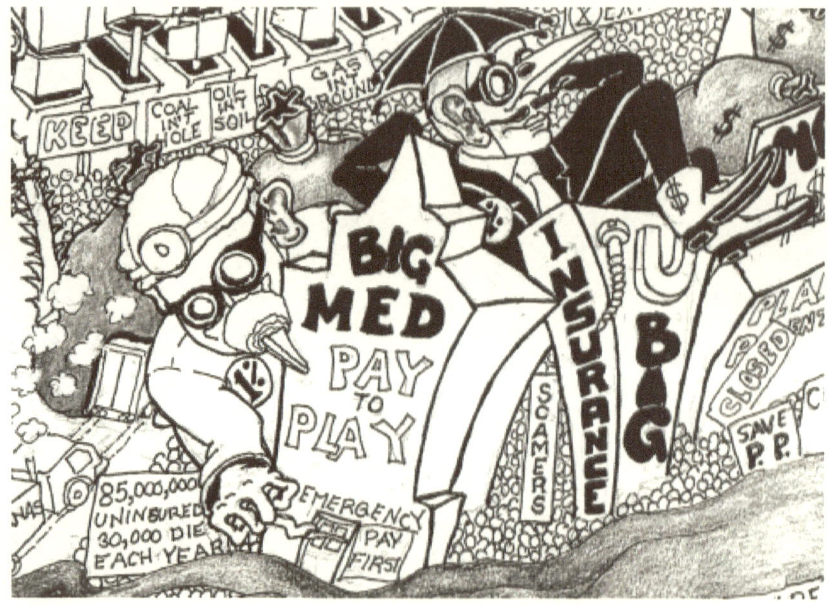

I wonder
If our ancestors had insurance at all?
What happened when from the tree they did fall?
What ambulance service could they call?
Who covered such a haul?
It could be
That indemnity started as a monkey's business
When bananas hadn't reached ripeness
And there was some bitterness
A smart monkey found a way to ensure sweetness
Or it could be
When cavemen were out hunting
And there was some question about sharing

That it often resulted in ranting
The biggest made an assessment, over their demanding
Even the Vikings
Needed a nullity against their banishing

A shield against eventual slashing
Even some sort of coverage against sinking

Most assuredly they had appraisals on mayheming
Probably the Egyptians
Took out a policy to offset the cost of entombing
Had a clause allowing for shrouding

But, allowing for the possibility of haunting

And left out, coverage against enslaving
We know the Romans
Would have had insurance, they invented legality
Built tall columns to support accountabilities
Created obligatory laws for new localities
Loved all things bureaucratize
The Spanish
Brought us demandable docility
Where the loss of life's security had inconsequentiality
But, by contributions of a gold commodity
Or an assurance of duplicity to severity could lead to cordiality
And now we have
Rationality replaced by litigationality
Our accountability becoming an enormous profitability

Our gullibility and laxity producing dishonesty without
modesty

Corporate ideology abandoning moral integrity

So where
Once, insurance was a safeguard and protection, a security,

    It has become part of a movement for Insatiable lucratively.

Concentrating on Medical emergence and necessity
In collaboration with Big Pharma and Big Med culpability

We now have
Disregard for mankind's, sovereignty

    Through civil appointee's corruptibility

Lost laws against accountability
Replaced with immunity for dishonesty
Even though
The cost of health is a calamity

    Congress continues to support profitability

And the greed of the one percent irresponsibility
Over the consequentiality to humanity
All of which
Could be fixed by relationality

    Where Congress could regulate insurance company's activity

Which dearly needs to become a reality
By enacting single-payer health for all humanity
Oh yes!
Who is going to pay for this novelty?

Why you are, of course! From the monies you pay them normally
Less the outrage of prices dumped on you under insurance captivity

Imposed on all of us by Big Med and Big Insurance originally,
It should be
That national health Insurance for all is free

In this situation, it would be standardized and easy for all to see
And if the government ran it collective bargaining would save us all money

And trying to understand it all would no longer be funny

BIG LOANS (PAY-DAY)

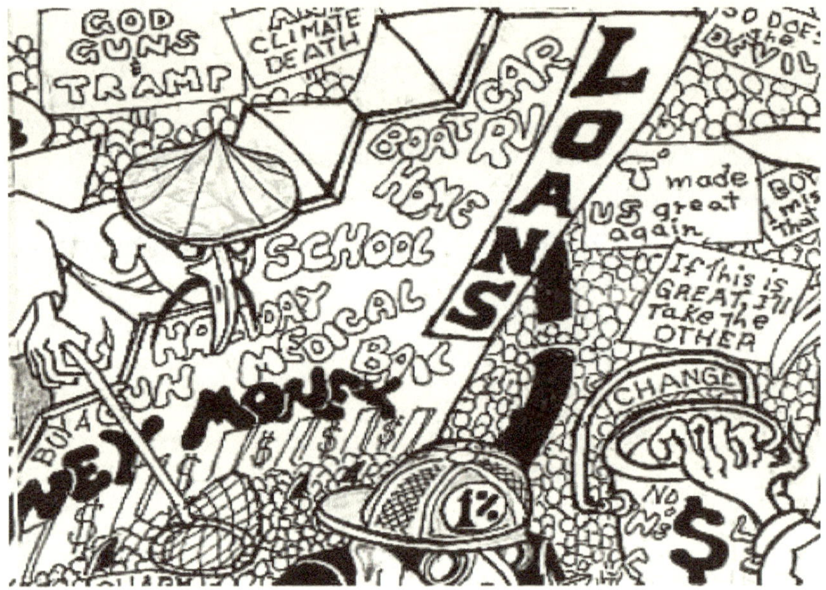

To be alone is when you need money (the most)
A sort of isolation brought on by desperation
Where to turn to find help, if you have friends or
not It can be a hole that closes over you
Being in the darkness
These moments often come without warning
Or they approach from a long way off
Money is such a cruel convention
If you don't have it when you need it
To find it is like digging a hole to China
Illness in your family and you can't cover the cost
You lose your job, Your unemployment runs out

You bought a car to get to work but can't make the payments
You are arrested and have to make bail
Your rent is killing you and you get behind
Ah, but pay-day loans are a trap
The money you may have to have
It sounds so easy, you are sure you will get it next week
And when not, you are looking at a lot more
And then it gets very messy, and being sassy, won't work
These loan sharks are protected by law but you are not
It is more like a form of gambling where the odds
Against you increase while you lose more and more
And what is it all for?
The greed for money just crawls out of every door

BIG WALLY

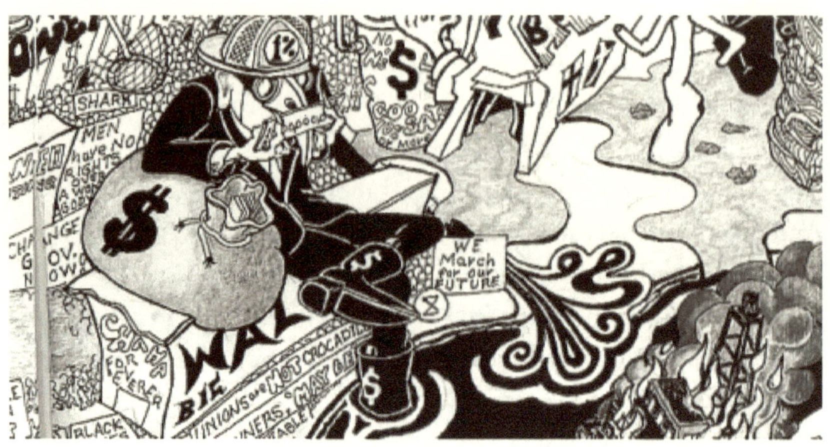

This isn't quite your normal family story about being poor
Though seldom bigger than a ballpark
With rows and rows of China's best, over which to pour
But, be assured this is no business, Lark
With stores all over this wide world
Between Big Wally and Apezon, the total market is their's to hold
o-o
All others seem to fail
Theirs is the tail that wags the dog
One with stores in every little dale
The others online the rest to hog
Both understand the principle of exploitation
Buy cheap from China, the money is in the importation
o-o
Never can it be said,
That they lead in any humanitarian way
Old folks mostly, who do the work, always minimally paid
While production is from countries far away

And on taxes, you guessed it
Seems they have friends, in the Senate
o-o
What about all those mom-and-pop shops
They can be bought for pennies on the dollar
Selling locally produced products, just pork chops
Is not 'American' anymore, If you have collared
The market in a big way, like Wally
All of this is a total folly
o-o
And I will tell you why,
If these big companies undercut their own people's production in the richest market in the world, they are in fact actively participating in the destruction of that economy by destroying its manufacturing base as well as its creativity and entrepreneurship.

People need to work to maintain themselves, of course, however, it is equally important to have a sense of worth about your job by knowing that you are helping to advance the conditions of life. A feeling that you are part of a creative whole for the betterment of society, Capitalism is rarely occupied by these thoughts and surly working for the advancement of one hugely wealthy individual or family falls short of this idea.

The ethic that one person or small group should have total control over the communal work of hundreds or thousands of contributors is a complete fantasy. It is a conception that is based on greed and false justification for the accumulation of vast fortunes. It is the reenactment of a feudal system that put land ownership over surfs. Simply another form of servitude.

This system is also leading to the destruction of the planet that we live on. There is no other world in reach, even as the one percent waste billions on this fantasy. We live on a very special planet that is being ripped apart in search of resources. Resources that in many cases are rare and limited for the sole purpose of making a profit. Government controls are limited and in many cases being reduced without real consideration. Because this scramble for resources is not for the direct benefit of the billions who inhabit this planet but solely for the accumulation of personal wealth this is a travesty against mankind and should be punishable. Governments have a responsibility to every person who inhabits this plant to control the extraction of resources for the future inhabitants and not to squander them for the benefit of a small class of ambitious billionaires.

When one percent of the population has more wealth than 60 percent, this is an economy that is draining the money that should be circulating. The government would normally collect taxes from the population and then return this money to the population in the form of public projects. Even the cost of running the government is put back in the form of wages. What is happening now is large amounts of money are being withdrawn from circulation by individuals and corporations. This can only lead to the ruin of all economies.

Corporations are owned by shareholders where the wealth is held as stock. When individuals accumulate large excess of money they can buy the stock until they control the sufficient majority and thus own and control the company. Corporations do the same thing, often buying their own stock until they have complete dominance. Workers on the other hand, although they helped create the wealth of the stock being held through ideas, labor, distribution or many other ways usually do not have options to buy stock. Normally their wages are minuscule in comparison to the collective value of the company. As the company increases in value, stockholders collect dividends which are similar to wages in that they are paid back for investing. Where workers invest their ideas and labor but only receive the wage the company sets for their help. A more equitable system would have the workforce represented on the board of directors of all companies and corporations and the creation of unions where workers actively participate.

When investors care they can sell their shares, usually at an increase in value while the worker can never do this. He has invested his creativity but has yet to receive a return on the success of the company and always can lose his job rarely being compensated for the loss.

Money makes money but it never creates anything but striff.

BIG CHURCH

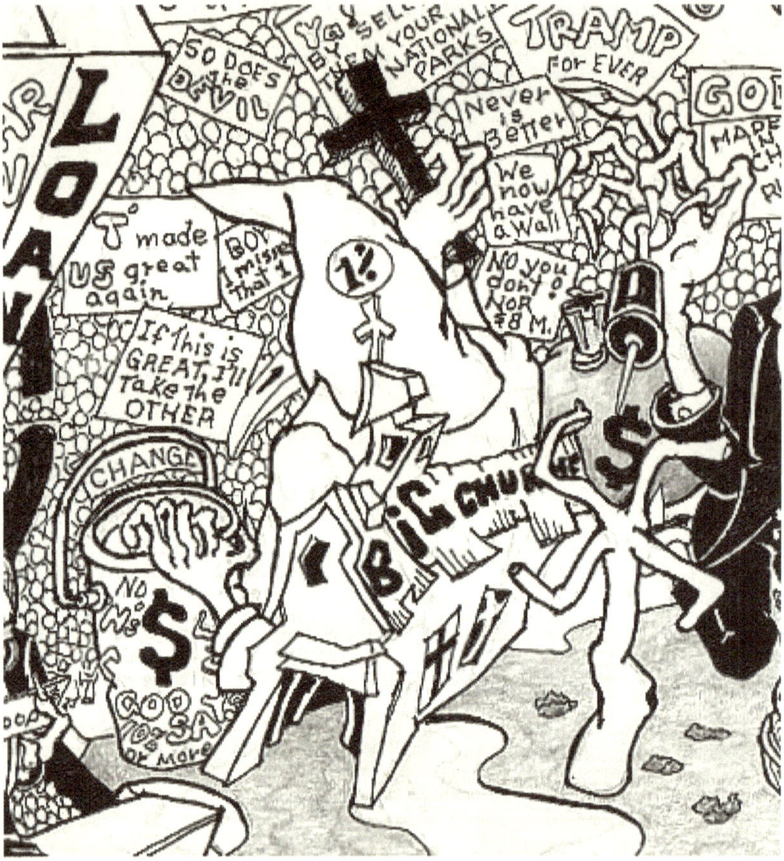

Surely, this is a posture that is reasonably right
But, churches have an open hand, that's tight
$$$
Asking for more than it's giving is the church's little secret, hidden
They pay no taxes on property and are not guilt-ridden.
$$$

Whatever they put their hand to, they are trusted
And for fraud, they are never busted.
$$$
It is a free ride to the pearly gates of wealth
But, best to buy that Gulf Stream with stealth.
$$$
It is so easy to help the church, just send a cheque
You will never see the Rolls with a speck
$$$
All those large estates serve to spread the word
To think this show of wealth is not needed, is absurd
$$$
Didn't Christ castigate the money changers?
Then he surely must love the money managers.
$$$
Clean is always how the church operates, especially in those Gulf states
You will never find a dirty clansman even if there is a bit of hate,
$$$
Does fire and brimstone on TV or on the pulpit open the mind to the
right power
Isn't it strange that racist or hateful folly should be taught under the
church's tower?
$$$
I once heard that Christ was poor but gave all he had to others
But, I am having trouble understanding how this church is making us
all brothers.
$$$
Is there not some confusion about money and power
These are never going to make your love a flower!
$$$
It all comes down to saying one thing,
While silently listening to the cash register sing,

$$$
The values of the church have not been lost
But so many millionaire clergies, have the wrong song
$$$
If a god made the earth as we are told
Why is the church not being bold
$$$
Pointing out there is no other earth to behold
Or was that never foretold
$$$
Our forthcoming countability makes it clear
That we should have been following Shakespeare
$$$

BIG MEAT

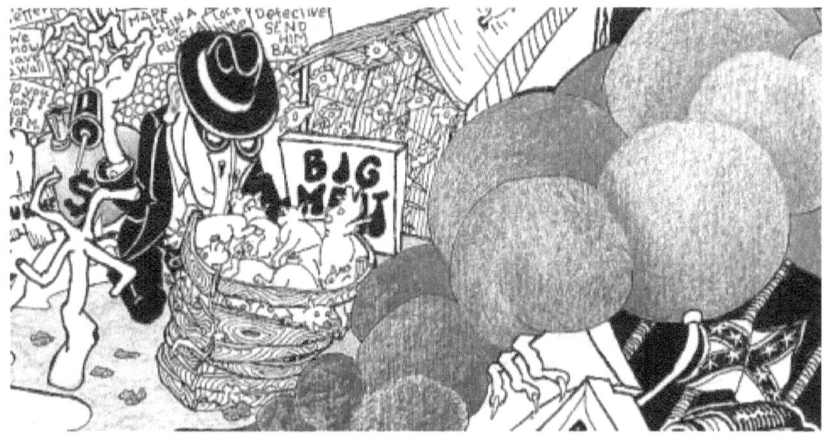

When our ancestors lived in trees
They ate flowers and greenery among the bees,
Until one day a monkey ate some bugs
That's when meat became a drug.

###

A rather silly move, to say the least,
For most big beasts, feast.
On greenie things, here and there,
And don't eat things that grow hair.

###

Some say it is the hunter's Instinct
That permits us to enjoy the stink
Like, when we eat, Tigers, Lions, Leopards, and those that stand tall.
The problem is they are all gone, because, we ate them all.

###

Wow, now stop, before you say
I just eat meat that eats grass or hay.
Sorry, that is no longer the occurrence
Now the meat you eat does not have this insurance.

###

Cows and pigs no longer live under the stars
But face life indoors, behind bars.
Gone are the pastures of recollection
Now it is total incarceration.

###

Animals don't dine among daisies
Or wear straw hats and visit Disney.
They are crammed into pens chaotic
And eat soya, steroids, and antibiotics.

Running free and skipping through the clover
All of that is over.
The meat of the future, thank God,
Will be grown in the lab unless it's a dog.

All of this could have a happy ending
And you'd be surprised how it would help your spending
If you just ate your spinach and artichokes
And thought of meat as just a joke.

Ah, then there are those wingy things
Like Schwarzenegger on steroids and also cannot sing.
Breasts like...well,...well, never mind,...hefty
With legs so thin, you could say they are flimsy

These poor creatures were once birds,
But men now raise them in their turds.
Pump them full of chemicals
Then stick them in cubicles.

Keep the lights on 24-7 so they can't sleep
All they have in their short life is to eat
Defeathered in a machine, soon after they are dead
Then tanked in bleach, to kill the bugs we dread.

You might think that Big Eats might have second thoughts
On how this cruelty could be blocked.
But no, the dollar shouts louder
Than any dead chicken from the larder

So here we are again, there is so much room for improvement
But when money is the sole employment
The solution gets stuck in bank accounts
With no accountability that counts.

Yet, so many of us keep chomping away
Not knowing, if what we ate, was nursing that very day
Never caring if what we ate ever got to sleep
With complete disregard for everything, except, if it was cheap.

BIG CON-STRUCTION

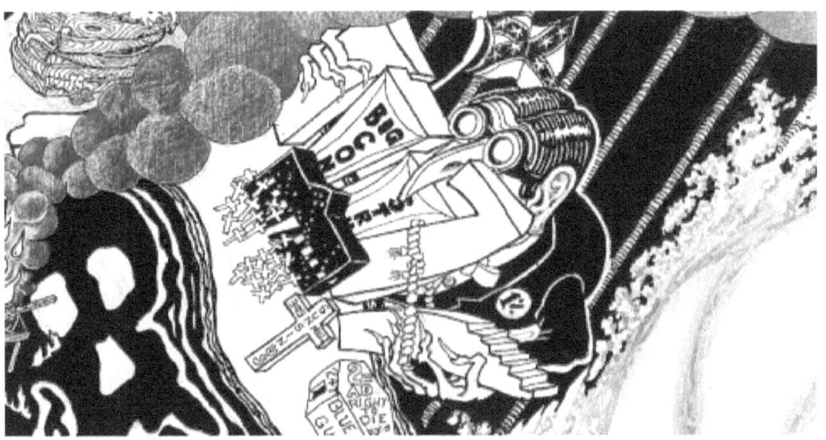

Bamboo shack on the beach
Is not where you find Big Money
These guys know where to reach
To tickle the monkey
%%%
Big Condominiums in a hurricane zone
sounds like just the right tone
Putting them together like chicken in a coup
Makes a lot of money in one scoop
%%%
Skimp, just a little, on materials
Will bring only a few funerals
But, never mind, money is what they are looking for
They are not interested in a durable floor
%%%
It's not just the retired, that they tackle

Big Con can be expected.to drop a billion and then cackle
On some old factory rejected, but now looks so fine
In some styles, no one can define
%%%
They could not care less
When It comes to houses for the homeless
Big Con is always out to lunch
It is something they won't touch
%%%
After all, money only helps those who have it
And, no one can be expected to share it
Yes, maybe a few bridges collapse
You can see their genius does not lapse
%%%
Big Con will tell you just how important they are
But, look at all those glass towers from afar
When it comes to monuments to the one percent
What is there to possibly resent
%%%
Now if you are looking for a house not very big
Boy, you are going to have to dig
Just an't no houses to find
You'r going to be in a real bind
%%%
Big Money has bought the lot
But, Big Tech will rent you a spot
You may have to pay dearly
But, you must understand clearly
%%%
It is not going to be cheap
But, don't make a peep
Because you will be on the street

Before you ever get to sleep
%%%
If you try to sell your old hand-crafted house
The agent will tell you it is the least valuable about
But you should understand that millionaires are made
From all those house owners who have been betrayed
%%%
Now you can see why so many are made to weep
Because to buy another house is way to steep
It is plain to see that to make money takes money
With no money the days are not going to be sunny

BIG OXY-CANDY

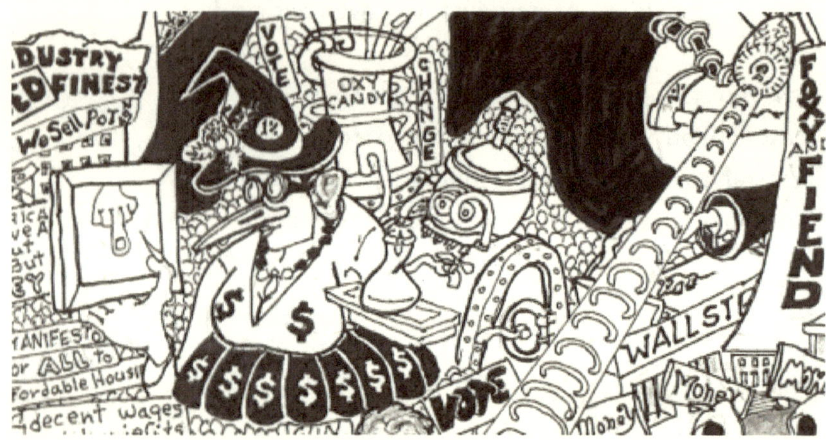

When the gods sprinkled the seeds of life
There must have been some strife
$$$
The little poppy with its flower bright
Has within its pod a gooey mess of blight
$$$
When men, looking for lunch, arrived
The little poppy made them blush and feel alive
$$$
What a wonder, how this dark sap does attack
A pleasant euphoria or thunder of wonder smack
$$$
But, all is not well, the little poppy's blood is black!
Humans gravel and desire more, when the poppy they lack
$$$
Oh gods, what have you done

The Devil has surly won
$$$
This Evil no one can see, but the cost is grave
When without, the mind, body, and soul will greave
$$$
Withdrawal is not some child's play
Pain and ack and sweat and tears enough to slay
$$$
So wicked are the effects, that one last hit is enough to die for
Oh, please just one to ease the pain and perhaps a very little more
$$$
It should be clear that in this little poppy, some danger is near
Stranger still, it is your fellow man you must fear
$$$
He who grew the poppy sells it to the next inline
And then the price just goes up until it is your time
$$$
It is hard to understand how other men would want to make you a fool
But greed is in the nature of so many, that you are just a tool
$$$
To gather money, the biggest evil of them all,
Which has no high, but the biggest fall
$$$
Yes, money, Money, MONEY, which turns men's hearts black
Your pain or death does not stop their attack
$$$
So you see, that the little poppy is just to enslave
This darkness has grown, so the poppy is just a wave
$$$
To be replaced, in the name of Corporate Greed
In billionaire lairs, the poppies madness, has been freed
$$$

Free from moral oversight, Oxy Candy now delights
Made in Corporate kitchens, for dollars ever so bright
$$$
Sold as a great relief from pain
When in fact your funeral is what will reign
$$$
Doctors, are not concerned with prices astronomical
Prescribe, without a sound methodology, the poppy pathological
$$$
One little pill and then another
Is the march to thunder
$$$
And whose idea is this? Why no less than the Corporations
Pharmaceuticals, that bring you all those medical preparations
$$$
You know, CEOs with big pockets that like art,
And their names on buildings, that never in public, fart.
$$$
But, it all comes down to Money, Why else would addiction
Be sold to those unknown, by prescription, really needs no encryption

FOXY & FRIENDS

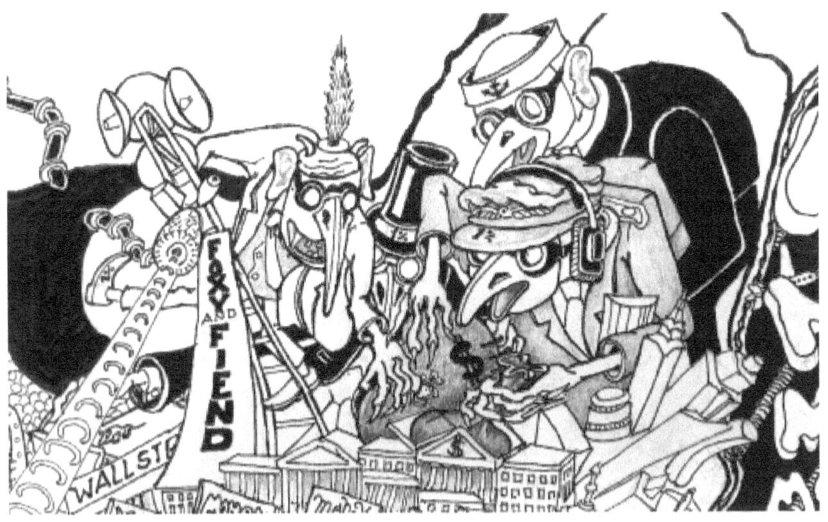

What a wonderful plaything, Money
The source of so much that's not funny.
With money, they can dance around the fire
While the whole world is just there for them to hire,

****

And what better way to play
To invent their own jaded truths to sway
Without much in the way of forethought
As something important but, really, naught

****

Then what is the news that Foxy and Fiends devise

If not a manipulative way, for more money to raise
Because with money they think comes power
And with power, they can become louder

****

Foxy and Fiends make it easy to understand
That louder is the way to undermine where others stand.
And every one of us should dread
A world of half-truths and where democracy is dead

****

The Money madness is driving the Fox
And they would have us all in that box
Nothing is acknowledged about fossil fuels
Renewable energy is for fools

****

Poverty is a lack of trying, and good work shipped to China
The underpaid is an illusion and not flat wages in Carolina
Big corporations shouldn't pay taxes, while their profits sore
It is left up to those who use axes, to carry the weight of the poor.

****

Big money expects it should make more and more
And when they have it all, they will explore ways to make even more
Foxy and Fiends stand by this atrocity
They would have you think, there is no better philosophy.

****

And who are these festy Fiends?

Why no other than the ones that glean by whatever means
Every last penny from the government, employees, and their staffers,
While they sit back and laugh along with all the other shafters

BIG FLY

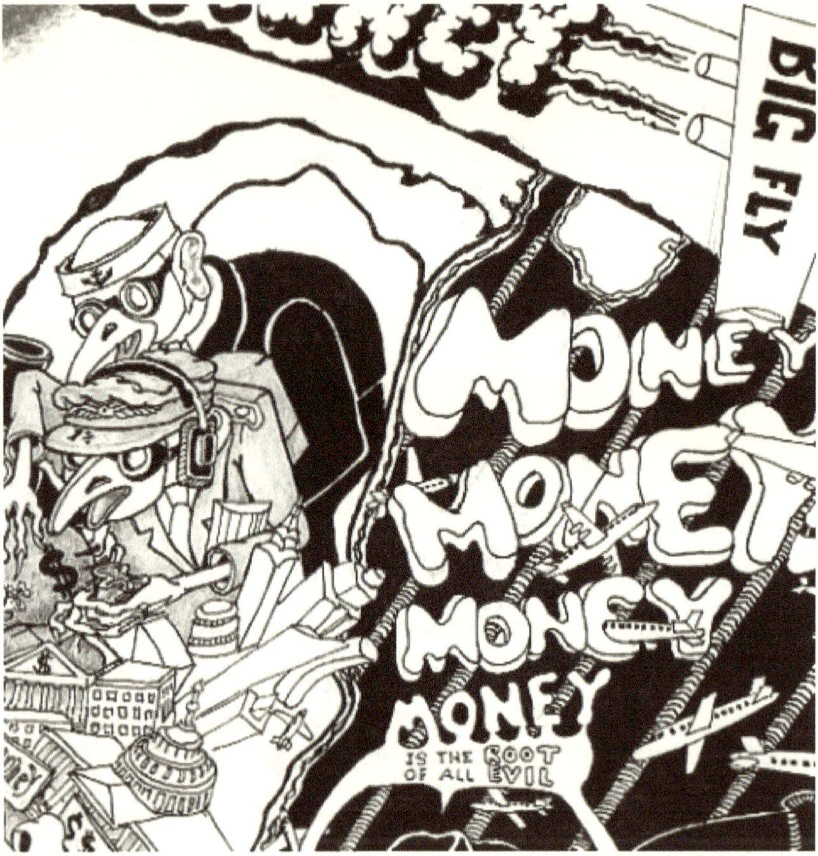

Big Fly is just a lie
Sit back and let me tell you, why

-o-

The airplane first to flight
Was built by the Brothers Wright

-o-

The motive, perhaps, was just delight
Sparked by the eagles floating slight
-o-
Of eagles and other birds of pray
Man has always wondered about their way
-o-
That birds use the air to play
But play is not what men best display
-o-
War, it is that makes them such a pest
For in war, he thinks that he is best
=o-
It is rather, that he is just a beast
And always first at the feast,
-o-
The big war made flying an itch
While putting so many in a ditch
-o-
Now, flying is not just about war
But, here, there is a lot to deplore.
-o-
It was plain to see the plane had a future
For making money it would be a mover
-o-
In the beginning, Aviation's mantra was service and comfort
But not now. Just to get into a damn seat takes effort
-o-
Where once planes got bigger and bigger
Why now you sit with feet around your neck is hard to figure
-o-
Who gets the armrest, the size of a pencil
And those knees in your spine are a hassle.

-o-
Worst of all is the food, which once had a taste,
Were now there is none, it is more a matter of time to waste
=o-
Shoulder to shoulder is fine, for marching
Getting a fork out of bulletproof wrapping is wishing
-o-
Have you ever dropped your pencil on the floor?
Or ever been able to get to the bathroom door?
-o-
After 10 hours in your box, oh, sorry, bucket
You land 5 miles from the exit,
-o-
Of course, you will have to hate
The couple of days you had to wait
-o-
For your bags. They went to New York
While your flight was rerouted to Old Cork.
-o-
Now of course, if you pay five times the price
You can sit in first class, with a Cuba libre on ice
-o-
More important than this wonderful flying
Is that you are participating in the earth's dying
-o-
Your carbon footprint just went through the sky
All those vaper trails are not a lie
-o-
Then there are the strange occurrences
Of multiple congressional tax deferences.
-o-
Is this the public paying twice?

Or just the usual thing, money as a vice?

-o-

So I will just say this! If you don't want to skip
That Tropical trip, just take a ship!

-o-

Of course, it's going to have to be one with sails
By the time you get there the weather will be gailes

-o-

As you can see, there are problems to resolve
Before many others evolve

-o-

Might be best to leave oil in the ground and walk
Big Oil and Big Fly are not going to talk

-o-

THE TRAMP

RESIST
US
Total GDP
$
TRAMP
ACKING
percent
SELLING
YOUR
ATIONAL
RKS
PH

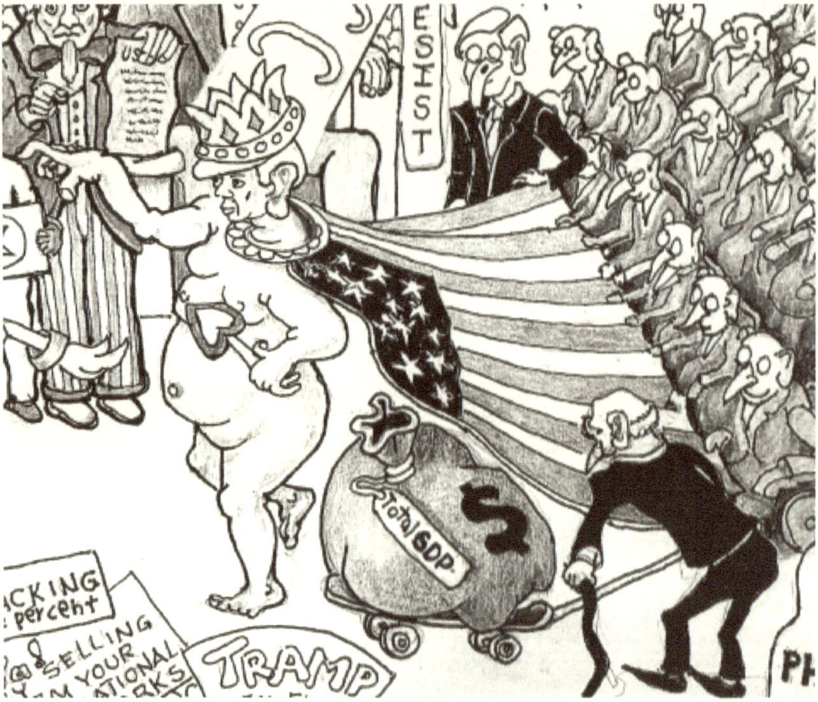

Oh yes, Ronald the 'Tramp' the want-a-be Emperor of the World. The little boy in a fat man's body can not see in his love mirror that he is not 'the fairest of them all'. Of course, the court of old republicans in the senate, who had long before he came along sold themselves to the devils of money, would not tell the truth to him. What a spectacle, parading before the world in his nakedness, expanding on his 'perfect genius' while tweeting to the world the ugliness that he saw in everyone but himself. The liar-in-chief of the 1%ers who, like them, had no sympathy for anything but money, and more money. I am sure that history will be divided, as our times are, over why humans have this strange nack of blindness to the evils of money. In my drawing, the Tramp has selected how to end the World from the Devil himself as he steps out of a tornado with his products for the apocalyptic destruction of the world but we already have everything except a plague.

???

His money given at his father's loss
Morals traded for wealth's gloss
Taxes masterfully dodged
Family continually robbed

???

His businesses started with promises
Money borrowed with pompous
Bankruptcies created with whimsy
Loyalties failed through folly

???

His women were placed as trophies
Indiscretions without pretenses
Allegations of scorn leave him unblushed
But monetary payoffs, well hushed

???

On TV, women he would flaunt
Usually, dressed in less than scant

While friend Epstein's desires hidden
He with daughters dances unbidden
???
Total Genius or ignoramus?
Artist of the Deal or Hippopotamus
College of Business or misconduct
Russian asset or just air duct
???
One thing we must all fear
Is a Tramp, who thinks, himself a Peer
To "make America great again"
Shouldn't include his financial gain
???
Democrats with Hillary, lose!
Democracy with Tramp is lost
Parties unchanged is the cost
Power politics are now the boss
???
The stench of violence he won
Over Hilary's righteousness shunned
Laws and friends now abused
While dictators are adored
???
Only fools vote for servitude
History shows it best to elude
Dictators throughout all time
Electing the Tramp was sublime
???
Flags waving, Republicans in step
March to change Democracy as kept
Democracy becomes hypocrisy
In the hands of an Autocracy

???
But, oh my god, the zombies arise
Like rednecks with apple pies
Guns n' roses, grab the ammo man,
Again, we march with the Klan
???
Now!, that there, is what life's about
The Tramp is our leader, without a doubt
Down with the "N's" and commies
And live by the cross and money's
???
Maybe the tramp ain't got much Money
But, he's full of self-serving honey
Rich suits think democracy's funny
Now are absolutely sunny
???
New national priorities hyped
Build a great wall, spiked
Immigrants with claims put in chains
Children are best in cages, for ages
???
Only the whites will get his consent
If death is a threat. no rules are bent
It is poverty's scent, he will resent
Destitution, in others, easy to accept.
???
While extreme wealth is adored
And opens all political doors
Poverty fines little or no room
Except in the dark damp tomb
???
Tramp as master of 'The Deal'

Canada pays more for steel
Harley's have lost a wheel
Mexico makes cars at a steal
???
China is putout to lunch
America will be the first to brunch
Though it doesn't make much
Profit is the most important crutch
???
Big money loves the Tramp
He allows no morals in the camp
Republicans at first worried
But, all have signed up in a furry
???
Smash those important world accords
New truths they can now record
Marches for racism to be the norm
While violence will be back in form
???
Racism has many, "very nice people"
"Black Lives Matter" should not be legal
Guns are every white guy's right
Children as victims, a small plight
???
Tramp's base, the working-class elite
Are happy to mix concrete
Education is a conceit
Own a gun, is a better receipt
???
Lifes work is, just to survive
Labor unions, commies contrive
Capitalism works, it will provide

Wealth to those who comply
???
One percent has it all, which means
Expect to pay more for blue jeans
The red party has money bags itchin
Big contributions don't need permission
???
The commies threaten to give money away
But, the Tramp will help stop that day
With a war, now isn't North Korea a bore
And, Uncle Putin is always at the fore.
???
Police keep killing more and more
Protesters into the streets pour
Civil protection looks like an intervention
While the rich undeeded subvention
???
Chemical agriculture sliding to starvation
Along with total environmental subjugation
As slavery replaces employment
World populations seeking redeployment
???
The Devil's Best Trick
And the Tramp is sure to pick
Is a killer Pandemic
Did he really choose an epidemic
???
The guy in the wig, says it's just play
The Chinese flue, it will go away
Don't be fooled, bleach is the tool
As thousands die, he looks like a fool
???

Pandemic, the devil's work is complete
Just in time to save the fool from a retreat
Close it all down, stay at home, it's airborne
Not from around here, got to be China-born
???
Billionaires and millionaire congressmen
Lead by counting their money like hens
Create their own science with half-truths
Fool everyone but our educated youth
???
Then came another damn election time.
With falts great and achievement lame
Tramp and party sense nullity
Twitter, rants show little sublimity
???
Only one way to stay elected
It worked to get him selected
Might work to get him re-elected
Might just get him one day convicted
???
Party in step, the Big Lie prepared
First, dig the trench, voting is impaire
COVID will stop the vote, much-disparaged
Machines rigged by satellites declared
???
The devil is said, to offer the sweet
Apocalypse only to the most elite
But, here we have the whole suite
Which one of them would he seek?
???
Of the four horses and riders
We have, the Atomic Annihilator

Chemical agriculture sliding to starvation
Along with total environmental subjugation
???
Postal Service slowed, word spread
Voting by mail, is not legal, alleged
Ballot made in China, all forged
Ah, but, Russia never mentioned
???
Now we know that he lost the race
But couldn't stand up to the disgrace
That doesn't matter to the Tramp
Using his favorite play, Lies Will trump
???
Elaborate prevarications stun the world
Dividing populations as the lies whirled
Democracy at the point of failing
While thousands attack Congress wailing
???
Absolute genius or not, the world awaits
Ninety-one indictments on his future fait
Half saying, "Tramp is our president"
Others saying, "Jail should be permanent"
???

CONGRESS

VOTING FOR ALL
NO GUN
VOTE
VOTE
RESIST
VOTE
SUN LAWS
PHARM LOBBY
OIL LOBBY
TECH LOBBY
MONEY
MONEY
"T" HAS BACKING OF THE ONE PERCENT
TRUMP FOR EVER
CHOOSE HIM

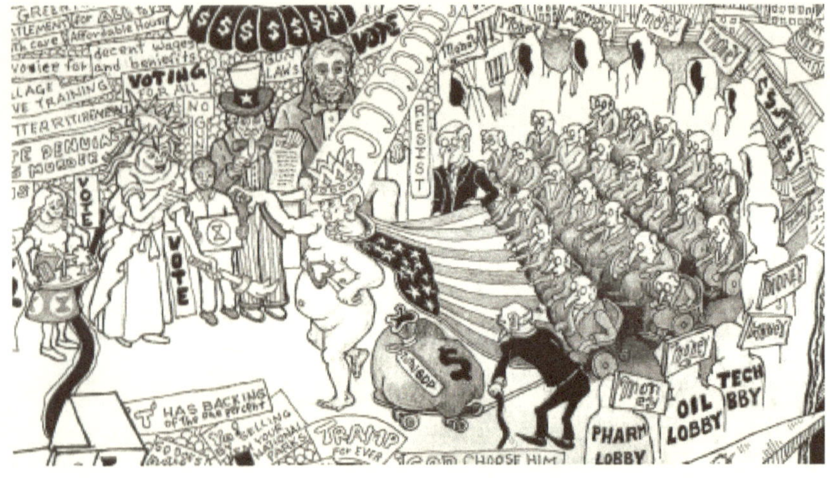

In the US the political system has just two parties, the GOP and the Dems. The problem with this is it polarizes the priorities of both parties. Changes can only take place when the will of the majority party wants them. This often centers around one vote while the total population of the US is 331.9 M people, only about 66% vote for primary elections. Most democratic countries have multiple parties where coalitions of different groups must agree to form an acceptable government if one party doesn't get a majority of all voters thus creating more cooperation within the government. In the US this is not the case and the GOP has managed to take down laws that protected the vote by allowing outside "Dark" money from millionaire individuals and corporations without declaring where it comes from.

The 1% in the form of individuals or corporations now have ways to influence the voters by saturating the public with un-vetted information supporting their wishes. Money talks louder the more you have to spend. As I am sure you can see, money gets people elected who then owe a large debt to those who financed their election. For example, the farmer who can get government subsidies to buy machines to produce food is more likely to be influenced by the candidate supported by the corporation making the machines than by a candidate who wants to help the unemployed farm worker survive. Or the chemical company that produces a questionable weed killer is given the ability to force its product on farmers through laws passed by Congress. This is our culture of MONEY.

At the time of writing, the GOP or Grand Old Party has the minority of one vote in the Senate while the Democratic Party's one-vote advantage is dependent on a millionaire who owns a coal-producing company and favors the GOP's outlook on just about everything, and was elected as a Democrat. It is sort of the case of the fox in the henhouse covered in feathers. This also helps demonstrate how divided the government has become. While the GOP is supported by very Big Money, the Democrats have a larger voter base. Although it is said that a majority vote determines US democracy, it is in reality, not. In general elections for the presidency, there is a second vote by each state's "Electoral Collage" where the rules are governed by laws in that state which can be influenced by the dominant party in that state. Trump tried to get some of these results changed where there was a GOP majority and may face laws against having done this.

This now brings us to the dilemma of our age. The structure of the US Democracy has falts that need to be clarified. The GOP has backers with tremendous amounts of money and power while The Dems depend on the voter to give them the power to make change. This struggle is a stalemate at the moment. With the general election coming up, this divide must be resolved. Big Money, Big News, and the GOP will spend while the Dems need your vote but, even more, your voice. The elections largely depend on the outcome of just a few states. The "swing states as they are known, are Arizona, Georgia, Ohio, Michigan, Nevada, North Carolina, Wisconsin, and Colorado where the vote may be very close and swing one way or another.

With this election being the most important for humanity in our lifetimes, It seems that in this day and age to get anything done we must melt cyberspace. Talk about it by putting your opinions up for discussion. If you believe that government should be a reflection of the needs of humanity you will be called a 'commie' and if you believe in the idea of a trickeldown government of the rich you will continue to be disappointed with the dictatorship that will follow. But whatever your thoughts might be, discussions during this election year must clarify the collective wish so that needed changes will be made. If we sit around while the climate crashes then so be it. Letting Big Oil dictate this decision is just not an option.

Another part of the US Congress is the Lobbyist. While there are 100 elected representatives in the Senate and 435 elected members in the House of Representatives, there are 12,000 registered Lobbyists who do not have to represent the citizens of the US and are not selected by them. The money that enters Congress through lobbying is estimated to be over

4 Billion dollars a year. Most of this goes to election campaigning.

Another feed into the system is the Political Action Committees (PAC) that are allowed to provide funds to help campaigns for or against candidates, ballot initiatives, and legislation, Much of this money comes from off-shore banks that are not always aware of where it comes from. Those who wish not to be known use these PACs to influence the government to do what they favor.

That leaves the voting public at a considerable disadvantage because the information that you need may be heavily biased. My feeling is that we all benefit from a universal understanding of what is right and what is wrong. We are all contained in our bodies and minds and depend on others to form our perspectives, but I think we instinctively know what is right and wrong. It is easy to understand that Global warming is from the wasteful use of a resource when there is renewable energy available and very positive possibilities for future development of these technologies.

We will soon be called upon to select a leader. If you think our political system is flawed, How do we select those to fix it? Since I created Money there have been new developments including creating non-profits concentrating on national and local issues. These start with local problems and some are expanding to a national level. The homeless issue throughout the US is a good example of where communities seek to find solutions and backing for these solutions within the community. Where Congress is slow or unable to overcome political blocks, this system is having good results. Young people are taking the oil corporations and state governments to court over inaction on the environmental issues they are blocking, with some success. The designers of the Constitution tried to design a system that would last, but that was a long time ago and it requires updating, and what better way than through public forums? These are exciting times.

Unfortunately at the same time, there are political elements that would change the system for their gains. Historically it seems that mankind buckles to the power of money. With human history full of kings, emperors, dictators, and military strongmen it should be clear this form of government isn't satisfactory, yet many fall for the illusion that one man or group is going to have the interest of all their subjects at heart. A benevolent dictator so to speak. The success of a democracy is its ability to deliver the best solutions for the collective good. This is of course not easy but having a lot of money does not impart this ability. Self-interest is a huge problem mankind faces. The best we can do is a collective approach that must strive to improve and not be prey to narcissistic groups with many complaints but no real workable solutions.

In this part of my drawing, I have included some well-known onlookers. From right to left is old ABE LINCON. Shockingly, he is the founder of the wheelchair group known as the Republican Party. What a change from the Emancipation Proclamation to the attack group on the Right to Vote. With a world population of over 8 Billion and growing, they want to ban abortions, there is no global warming, strip-cut the world forests, and support the Tramp's whims.

Next is UNCLE SAM, once the beloved symbol of US Democracy. Now an aging figure of indecision and strife.

This young lad represents the MINORITY GROUPS of the US. White some would have you believe that being 'white' is somehow the right color for the US while we all know that the Americas were conquered and overrun a mere couple of hundred years ago by marauding warriors from a different continent searching for gold (money).

LIBERTY needs no introduction and a tried and tested figure in the continual fight for the liberty of all mankind. Not a supporter of the Tramp or the GOP in its present form but has stood at the gates of this country welcoming immigrants from all over the world. Certainly as well known as Gabrial at the gates of Heaven.

Next is GRETA THUNBERG, a young Swedish Climate Change activist who has inspired worldwide resistance to the pollution of the world's atmosphere. Her remarks are of a quality that has put her far above the trolls working for climate denial. The climate issue was first reconciled some 60 years ago and has been steadfastly resisted by Big Money for all that time. In the '60s there was a lot of concern about the world population increase but this was also resisted by those that foresaw the prospect of huge capital increases worldwide that would follow. The basic concern then was that with a huge worldwide increase in demand for earthly resources, there would come a time when humans would have to return to stone age living. In the 60s we didn't fully understand what the car was doing.

In the 50s in Los Angeles where I grew up, we had smog alerts when it got so bad that it was hard to see two cars in front of you. Big Oil knew that they were killing us but, you know, there was a lot of money to be made. Big Car reluctantly put "devices" on their cars as they made them bigger than ever. Public transport became millions of miles of concrete and 'black top'. On the rare times that you could see it, LA merged with the sea and the sunset was always a yellow circle in a red sky.

In the 60s Buckmiserter Fuller began to pour sensible ideas into our smoggy eyes with statements like, "You can make money or you can make sense, the two are mutually exclusive" and "Humanity is acquiring all the right techniques for all the wrong reasons". But, "Bukky" Fuller's gem was the idea that humans change only when a better idea is presented. Seeing the Earth as a "Spaceship" goes a long way in pointing out the faults of Capitalism as a model. The spaceship also allows for the change of the concept that a God made the earth for us to a more rational idea the earth is god. Not God as a noun but rather an interactive system that supports life that we collectively must cherish and understand that its well-being is paramount to our existence.

With the huge unbalance of money that I have presented here, it is clear that the 1% know the resources on earth are finite and are pouring the world's wealth into start-up space travel companies that use these resources to go to other satellites of our sun to look for what is being used up by themselves. Space travel to rock piles to make them like Earth? No! To bring back handfuls of resources to replace what they are using? No! To make more money? This is clearly, the wrong model for our sustainability here on Earth.

CREDITS

Operating Manual For Spaceship Earth - R. Buckminster Fuller, Southern Illinois University (1969)

The Meaning of the 0th Century - Kenneth Boulding, (1964)

Essay (Economies of the coming Spaceship Earth - Kenneth Boulding, (1966)

The Closing Circle - Barry Commoner, (1971)

The Limits of Growth - D. Meadows, Dennis Meadows, Jorgen Randers, and W. Belarans (1972) - (12 million copies worldwide)

Only One Earth - Barbara Ward, Rene Dubos, (1972)

Gaia Hypothesis - Lovejoy, (1972)

Cradle to Cradle - William Mcdonald, Micheal Braungart, North Point (2002)

Big World Small Planet - Jhoan Rockstrom, Mattias Klum, (2002)

Shirking the Earth - Oxford Uni Press, (2016)

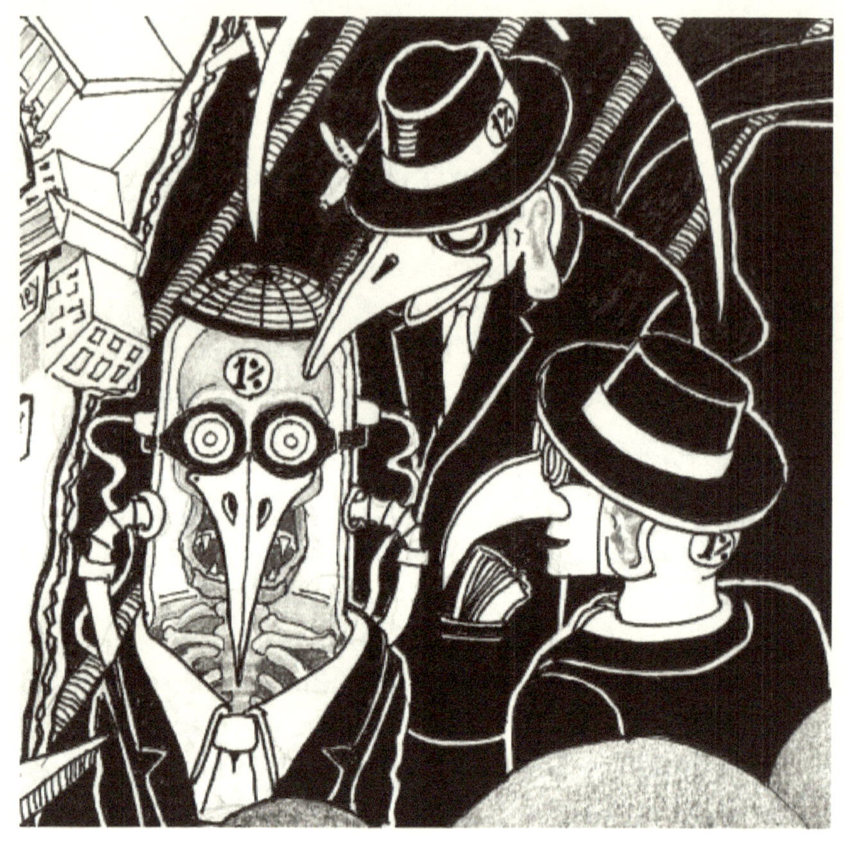

Money, Money, MONEY,
The Real Pandemic, The 1%
By Steven Selby

www.ingramcontent.com/pod-product-compliance
Lightning Source LLC
Chambersburg PA
CBHW031744150726
47989CB00006B/2593